SUFFOLK
TALES

SUFFOLK TALES

by

H. Mills West

COUNTRYSIDE BOOKS
NEWBURY, BERKSHIRE

First Published in 1982
by Barbara Hopkinson Books
© H. Mills West 1982
This edition published 1989

COUNTRYSIDE BOOKS
3 CATHERINE ROAD
NEWBURY, BERKSHIRE

ISBN 1 85306 036 4

Produced through MRM Associates, Reading
Printed in England by J.W. Arrowsmith Ltd., Bristol

Contents

Foreword

In these short tales I have tried to recall the kind of people we were once in East Anglia and the kind of life we lived before the veneer of modernity came to blur the charm of separate identity in both person and place. All of the tales have appeared in the East Anglian Daily Times as 'stories' though what I have been concerned to do was merely to capture a glimpse, story or not, of times that are gone and already fading from human memory. Most of them are wholly or partly true, all, I believe, are of the essential quality of old East Anglia.

H.Mills West.

Martin and the Kaiser

Martin took a pitch-fork from the corner of the barn and went out into the harvest field. The yellow stubble was short and hard against his boots; after the sheep folds and the smell and blaring of sheep he welcomed the stubble, crunching it under his feet as he walked across to join the men.

It was better than sheep, he thought, working on the arable with the men and the waggons, but when you were fourteen and even smaller than fourteen suggests, you had to go where you were told.

"Well, here come the good shepherd hisself", one of the men said as he came up to them and one or two men laughed good-humouredly without stopping their work.

They were loading one of the waggons with wheat sheaves, two men on each side and one aboard, and they jabbed their forks easily into the crisp, gold straw of the leaning sheaves one by one and lifted them high above their heads.

The task was familiar and satisfying to them. The sheaves rose and sailed through the air and subsided upon the edge of the waggon where Jim the loader frantically speared them again to move and arrange them for a proper load. Jim looked as busy and anxious as if he were building a cathedral with his own hands, striving to keep the corners built up and the sides even and he would put a load on the waggon as big and as steady as a small stack.

1

Martin began to use his pitch-fork with the others - enjoying the movement and the feeling of strength in his muscles for all his diminutive proportions - but Jim shouted worriedly from the top of the load:

"Not another one a-loadin'? I can't do no more'n I am!"

"Martin", said the foreman, " - tell yew what. Yew c'n lead ef yew like. That'l help all on us 'en."

Martin came round to the front, proud and conscious of the power and the manliness of the occasion with the great horse and the waggon and the men depending on his lead.

Barely high enough to take the rein beside the slavering mouth and bright steel bit, he contrived to bring the horse along between the rows of shocks, leaning well away to avoid the huge splaying hooves.

When the waggon came abreast of standing shocks he would shout and pull his weight on the greasy rein and astonishingly the great beast would stop and pant and turn its head to nudge him and see what kind of midget was there. The pitch-forks would flail on both sides of the waggon and the yellow sheaves form higher and higher arcs and it was time to move on again.

Martin would gather all the importance of his task into a high-pitched yell:

"Hold tight!". Then, when the load became so big that even Jim had to call a halt, there would be ropes flung over and made taut.

Martin would climb up the ropes to the very top and cling there against the moving sky as the load of sheaves rolled and billowed, sliding along under the clouds until there was no account of time or distance

- then suddenly the movement stopped and below was the familiar stackyard and the men looking up as they took off the ropes.

"He can take the loose hoss back to the fi'ld", someone said.

The horse was out of the shafts and standing immense in its accoutrements. "Up yew go", and the horse's back appeared acres-broad and cluttered with harness. Martin half-turned to ask a question but the horse was already moving. It carried him out of the yard and into the lane. It was like being a king, he thought, high up on the great horse that was his servant.

As he got back to the field a rabbit broke cover from a shock and a boy clubbed it with a knobbed stick and took it to join the row of bodies under the tree. At the end of the day he was given one of the rabbits and he carried it home dangling from the stick over his shoulder.

He walked with the rabbit through the evening fields and felt proud with his tiredness. It had been a wonderful day and his triumph was there on his stick for all to see.

It meant nothing to Martin beside such pleasure that this self-same summer day was that on which a war began against the Kaiser Bill. Come what may, he determined, he would be a horseman: blow the Kaiser.

Next day the foreman looked doubtful when Martin enquired of him the chances of working with the horses. He appeared to consider the matter, for he knew how important horses were to a boy, but he could not help smiling at Martin's stature.

"Tell yew what," he said at last, "I'll keep yew in mind to help owd Bob with his pair jist as sune as yore man enough. Can't say fairer 'n 'at, can I? As sune as yew c'n harness a hoss an' yore man enough to look arter it, well then, yew can work it."

It was fair enough but well-nigh impossible for Martin, as he knew, but he was so set upon the prospect of horse work that he determined to show what he could do. Next morning he arose and went through the cold half-light at half-past four in order to get to the stables before even the first horseman should arrive. The docile Prince was there in the middle stall of seven and he threw a hand-cup full of oats into his trough and saw the great bronze head come forward into the lamplight. Martin struggled to lift the huge collar on to the edge of the manger beside the champing jaws and clambered up himself, holding the collar inverted on the wood, knowing that if he could get the collar on he would have won. But the weight of it with the metal hames and hanging chains was all he could manage - to push it over the moving, uncooperative head seemed impossible. Time after time he lifted the collar but the head drew back and he lost balance himself and had to climb back again.

Yet when hope was nearly gone the horse seemed to submit, held its head still and firm, and in the very act of overbalancing again Martin slipped the collar over its head and managed to turn it right way up. With muscles aching and face covered in sweat, he looked up in triumph when the horsemen came in. The foreman was with them. When they saw what Martin had achieved they stared at him and at each

4

other in a sober silence. The foreman put his hand on Martin's shoulder.

"Yew done that well, bor," he said, "- trouble is that don't 'mount to anything now. The Army - they're a-takin' the hosses cos o' the war."

Martin's chin sank to his chest but he did not know he was crying till the drops fell on the straw at his feet. He was ashamed but could not stop. "Yew git along hoom, bor," the foreman told him. "We c'n git on 'thout yew for a little while."

But Martin hung about the farm and felt the strangeness that had suddenly come upon everything. It was an astonishing thing to see that the men were not setting out to the fields but standing about in the farm buildings as if uncertain even of the daily routine that had been part of their lives.

When the foreman came back from consulting the boss, they all gathered in the barn, twelve men and two boys all told, and sat about awkwardly on the straw. They were embarrassed at meeting together and not doing anything with their hands. They pulled at the straw for pieces to pick their teeth.

"Well I s'pose that ain't tew bad," the foreman said doubtfully. "They're a-goin' to leave us tew o' the hosses for now - owd Boxer an' Lady - so as we c'n manage the muck cartin'. But some o' the land 'll atter go down to grass, the boss say. So that look as if some on us 'll atter go".

In the silence of the barn one of the horsemen cleared his throat.

"We're a-goin'," he said. "We decided that a'riddy. Jim an' me an' Charlie, we're a-goin' to join up. That ain't no use us a-hangin' on heah 'thout no hosses."

Martin felt as if the world was splitting and disintegrating inside the quiet barn. The foreman had more to say:

"We gotta take the hosses to the barracks ourselves. I know that ain't much of a job. Tha's bad enough losin' the hosses 'thout havin' to hand 'em over. The boss say 'haps some o' yew 'll volunteer. That need three men an' a waggon."

"I'll take tew," said Martin in a voice he could scarcely realise was his own. "I'll take Prince an' lead another."

The foreman looked at him. "I ain't callin' on yew, Martin," he said kindly, "- but o' course yew did put his collar on. Yew go ef yew like. Yew ride Prince and lead Sally - come back on the waggon."

Martin found himself in the stable again and this time there were others to lift the heavy collars and britching. When they gave him a leg up to straddle the broad back, the great bronze head turned to question. He shook the reins and rode on Prince like a king to execution along the lanes and into the streets and over the cobbles of the barrack square. He slid down from the height and handed the reins to a man in a uniform whose face he could not bring himself to look at and left Prince and ran.

To the end of his life he could not remember the rest of that day, though he had a recollection of going back to the farm sitting on the tailboard of the waggon. He felt very cold and he wanted to get into his bed and go to sleep.

Grandfather's Wages

One Saturday after the disastrous harvest of 1896, my grandfather, who was the head horseman on a farm in the Waveney area, came home to his cottage without his wages. It was six o'clock in the evening and Grandmother and the whole brood of ten children were waiting to begin the meal of dumplings and rabbit stew.

Throughout the meal Grandfather ate in silence thinking of the long week he had worked and of the feckless character of his employer who had doubtless gone off on a drinking spree and forgotten to pay him.

Afterwards he sat in his chair by the fire for a time, wondering what he should do. Grandmother brought out the flour sack from the pantry and showed that it was quite empty. She had used the last cupful or two for the dumplings, she said; there was no bread in the house and not a mite of anything to make a meal.

"That fare to me I atter work for my wages and then fight for 'em," Grandfather grumbled. "But don't yew worry. Yew git yar baking tins riddy - I'll git some flour somehow." He put on his coloured neckerchief again and Grandmother brought his heavy boots and buskins.

Five or six of the children swarmed behind him as he left the cottage and walked down the loke to the farm. There, he harnessed one of the horses to a waggon while the children clambered up over the sides and sat on the floor. Grandfather threw an armful of meal sacks into the waggon for them to sit on, and set off to find the farmer.

It was a late September evening and fine and dry. For several miles the children were in high spirits but as the dusk came down they began to huddle together in the sacks. Before the waggon had reached Bungay, it was quite dark. Grandfather knew there was a public house there that his employer frequented and after some enquiries, found out where it was. Grandfather pulled the waggon into the yard and got down.

Although it was an inn where labourers were not welcome, Grandfather walked straight in and searched through the public rooms only to be told that the farmer had moved on to another public house outside the town. After enquiring from passers-by Grandfather managed to locate the inn and there discovered his employer in the tap-room with a group of cronies.

"Evening Master," said Grandfather with a respectful firmness, "I'd like my wages, if you please." Half stupefied the farmer stared at him.

"Hev you come all this way jest for that?" he asked at last. "You could 'a' had it come Monday."

"I got 12 mouths to feed," answered Grandfather. "They don't stop eating on Sunday."

Some of the farmers began to make comments about paying wages at the proper time. Grandfather's boss took him aside.

"Tha's a rum job tonight," he said. "I'm nearly spent out. Are you right out, then?"

"There ain't a bite in the house. A couple of stone of flour would tide us over."

8

"Well I'll tell you what to do. You go along up to Jackson's mill over in Ashington. Ask him for a sack of flour and tell him it's for me. Do you try that."

Grandfather had a rough idea where Jackson's mill was but there wasn't much light to go by except the stars and a candle lantern each side of the waggon, and the journey seemed to continue for miles along strange roads and dark country lanes before he found the place. The children were quiet, as miserably tired of the endless jolting as of the cold, but they roused themselves to peer over the side of the waggon as the miller came out.

The miller was carrying a lantern and lifted it to look at Grandfather as he explained his errand. When he heard the name of the farmer he became angry. "He's got no right to send you over here for flour. He owes me money. I can't afford to supply him with goods he don't pay for."

Grandfather was too proud to beg. He walked stiffly back to the horse and had begun to turn the waggon around when the miller caught sight of half-a-dozen small white faces looking at him over the side.

"Howd yew hard, mister," he called to Grandfather. He came closer and shone the light into the children's faces. They were pinched and still with cold and fright. He stepped back and said in a different voice. "Ef you back yar cart up to the barn door I'll give you a sack of flour and welcome. But git them poor little owd kids hoom in the warm."

With the sack of flour and an old tilt that the miller had stretched over the children in the waggon, Grandfather set off on the journey home. By the time he had got back to the farm it was nearly midnight. He bedded the horse down and carried the flour on his shoulder to the cottage.

Grandmother had got the oven going and the tins were warming in front of the kitchen range. Without a word she got to work on making dough and none of the children - save the youngest - was rash enough to ask for food before they went to bed. For the youngest Grandfather took a penny out of his pocket and asked him if he wouldn't rather have the penny than supper. In the morning Grandmother would recover the penny by offering the "biggest" breakfast in exchange.

Grandfather stayed up in the kitchen until the smell of the fine new loaves began to fill the house. With luck there would be another rabbit in a snare come daylight and the family would have full stomachs when they went to church.

Sunday Arternoon

On Friday was the wages, on Saturday evening the pub, but on Sunday - that was the day for courting. When you went courting for the first time the village women would note the fact, screwing up an eye and nodding their heads knowingly.

To prove that you meant nothing you walked as far away from the girl as possible without actually leaving her company. Nevertheless, you were held to be "sweethearts" and sure enough you joined the other couples redolent of lavender water and summer posies who strolled the footpaths through the fields or sauntered along the lanes or river banks.

As time went by, the gap between you and the girl would lessen and when you became a fully-committed lover you would put a proprietorial arm around her waist or walk arm-in-arm in full view.

One of the latter kind was Freddy Finch, who worked on his father's smallholding. Freddy was a respectable young man of serious intent - one who, after long practice, had become an accomplished and even elegant stroller.

His initiation had begun six years before when he had been allowed to join Elsie's large family on one of their Sunday afternoon walks. On that day he walked in Elsie's company for the first time. It was a meagre triumph, in fact, for apprentice as he was, he had to pretend to the remainder of the family that Elsie's presence was merely fortuitous to his natural

11

ardour for walking. But it was a beginning.

Looking back Freddy had to admit that progress had been slow, even after he and Elsie began to walk out on their own. Perhaps he was not really a born stroller and found it difficult to believe that you had to walk such a very long way to capture a maid. Perhaps it was a reluctance to commit himself to the village folk who were his neighbours. To them it was one thing to be "going out" with a girl and quite another to be "courting strong". Once you were "courting strong" your status was crystallised by village opinion into an almost inextricable compromise. It was a situation not lightly to be entered into.

Nevertheless by the spring of 1922 Freddy and Elsie were "courting strong", all restraints and subterfuges were put aside. He walked openly with his arm round Elsie's waist which was never a completely happy achievement for they could never adapt their steps to each other and were constantly jogging and bumping at the hips. The message, however, was clear. Freddy had walked himself to the altar - almost.

Unfortunately, there is a tide in love affairs which can leave one high and dry if not taken at the flood. Perhaps a single word spoken during the heady days of the previous summer when they cycled to Felixstowe and back for each of the three days of their holiday would have carried them headlong into blissful matrimony. Nothing was said.

By the spring a slight sourness had crept in, despite the recognition that they were "courting strong". There was a certain unwillingness to set off on long walks; a mutual agreement that some of the foot paths and lovers' lanes were so familiar that they were likely to sink into hysteria if they had to walk them just once more.

By the end of June things had come to a head. On Sunday, the 18th, Freddy turned up for the first time in five years without a flower in his buttonhole - on the following Sunday without a buttonhole or gloves. The end came on July 2nd, when they agreed to take a short cut. It was against all the traditions of courting. They arrived back at little more than mid-afternoon and could not face the thought of setting out again. They separated.

The rift became complete during the next few weeks. Freddy worked harder on the smallholding than he had ever worked before and calculated as he worked the number of miles he had walked for nothing, the gross weight of all the bags of buttered brazils he had squandered his money on, and all the time that he could have spent doing something else. Elsie spent her Sundays helping her mother in the house and making Suffolk rusks.

After a few weeks Freddy became friendly with a girl who cycled. She had a beautiful new bike with skirt guards and a basket in front. Freddy cleaned his own bike and added an acetylene lamp. For three Sundays they whirled along the country roads and Freddy thought how pleasant it was to travel so far afield. He had to admit, however, that it was purely a relationship of fellow travellers. She seldom dismounted - and rode fast along country lanes where there were stiles or places to sit. Freddy followed behind and thought how beautiful she looked when he could see her.

In the meantime, Elsie had gone out a couple of times with a cousin of hers who had a rowing boat at Woodbridge. On a Sunday afternoon he would row up to Kyson Point or even to Waldringfield if the tide was right. It was such a pleasant change, thought Elsie, and so healthy.

She wore a long white dress and a straw hat that tied under the chin with a pink ribbon in case the breeze was strong. She sat in the stern seat while her cousin rowed and grimaced and got stuck in mud banks, and she repeatedly smiled whenever he caught a crab and the water doused the front of her dress. The third week she declined the invitation and stayed at home to make rusks.

It was the same Sunday on which Freddy had decided to retire from a back view of his lady-friend cyclist. He was cleaning out the poultry huts when he happened to look along the lane and saw Elsie coming with a basket.

At first sight he was in a panic to hide. For one thing, he was wearing his old dungarees and without collar and tie and Elsie had never seen him like this in her life. For another, he had a sudden, unhappy vision of starting the courtship all over again. If they made it up they would have to go walking out again, and at the thought of the endless round of lovers' lanes and winding footpaths, the double-breasted suit and the buttonhole - and the buttered brazils - his heart sank. Never again, he thought, not on these legs.

Elsie came into the gate of the smallholding and went up to the house. Freddy watched from the poultry houses and saw his mother come to the door. His mother was shaking her head and pointing and there was Elsie coming towards him. He stepped out of the shed knowing it was hopeless to look anything but dirty, untidy and utterly beyond restitution.

"Hullo Freddy," she said, and he knew by the casual voice she was not in the mood to think about courting again. "I want some eggs - for rusks."

"Eggs for rusks?" he said stupidly. There was some flour on her forehead. He took the basket into the shed where the rows of nests were. There were some hens on the nests and he put his hand under carefully to find the newest eggs. They were warm and brown and had bits of straw clinging to them. Elsie was standing there watching.

"I used to do that when I was a little girl," she said. "I think that's one of the nicest things anyone in the world can do - get eggs out of warm nests." She wasn't using her courting manners and he knew that was over for good. He forgot he was dirty.

"Yeah, tha's nice," he agreed. "Collectin' 'em in a pail."

"Or in a basket - a basket full of eggs."

"I know what yew mean." For a few moments they were both lost in nostalgia.

"I'd take it kindly," he said, "ef yew'd come sometimes to collect the eggs - while I'm cleaning 'em out, like."

"Every evenin'," Elsie said. "In my oldest clothes."

"Don't forgit to bring some o' yar rusks," Freddy told her.

Reuben

I remember Reuben, though it is more than forty years since I saw him. He used to sit in a wheel-back chair in the porch of his cottage. Despite the labouring life he had led, he had the peculiar ability of the Victorians to present an appearance of patriarchal respectability.

As a child I saw him often; I knew the cottage and the church nearby and the sandy lane that led to the main road. There was something stolid - or stoical - in the way the lonely old man sat upright and still, holding his stick between his knees and looking into the distance.

It was not until he died that I came to know of the griefs that must have plagued his thoughts in his old age, for I was given the scraps of papers and the Family Bible that was the family's history.

Reuben had married in 1866, soon after the harvest. On a fine autumn day he and his bride walked the short distance from the church to the cottage that was to hold them for the rest of their lives. No doubt that it was a happy day, no less because he served the land and a good master, for this was still the golden age of farming. It is no satisfaction to know now that the times were rapidly changing for the worse and that the clouds of rural depression and of dire want were gathering behind them on that day.

Twelve children were born in the four-roomed cottage. The first was Emily, destined to be the second mother and a tower of strength both to her parents and to the younger children. It was on Emily, responsible and sensitive as she was, that the shame and privation of the lean years must have fallen the heaviest. When she was two years old the law was passed making school attendance compulsory and when the new village school was built she became one of the first pupils. Emily, in fact, became a model pupil, a joy to the teacher and a trusted monitor at the age of nine. At the same age she helped the school cleaner to dust and scrub for a wage of sixpence a week.

By this time she was dragging behind her to school four or five of the younger children. Generally, she led them by way of the lane and the row of cottages in a respectable manner but sometimes in the summer she was persuaded against her better judgement to take the grass-grown track known as the Church walk. It was always held that this was a short cut but the real attraction lay in the taste of the forbidden. From the Church walk they would have to enter the churchyard and cut across between the melancholy rows of stones, then skirt the church porch with footsteps placed very quietly on the gravel. The final part of the journey was a wild scoot across the paddock in front of the Rectory, in a delicious fear that the Rector - or worse, his wife - would be watching from the windows. They were in fact, never seen; or if seen, never reprimanded.

To Reuben and his wife, life became a struggle to keep the whole family from being sent to the workhouse. The desolation of the 'eighties and 'nineties. with falling farm prices and the lowering of wages, was miserably reflected in the lives of the family in the small cottage. An extra burden that was difficult to bear was the paying of school pence. Twopence a week had to be found for each child and whilst the money could be saved for this, Emily would carry it carefully to school each Monday morning.

The time came when the school pence could no longer be found. There was an investigation and afterwards the charge was made on the Union. Once a quarter the clerk from the workhouse paid the money to the school, and for all Reuben's efforts, the transaction was known. It was a stigma - the smell of the workhouse was upon them all. It was in shame at this, rather than at their ragged clothing, that made the children take the lonely short cut more often.

So it was that, as the children became older, the short cut was revealed as having another advantage: you could reach the turnpike as well as the school without being seen by the village people from their cottage windows. When they were only 12 or 13, two of the boys, unable to face the scorn of their contemporaries over the Union payment of the school pence, and seeing no end to the poverty at home, put a few belongings into a coloured handkerchief and took the shortcut before daybreak one morning. What privations they knew is unrecorded but they were picked up three weeks later as waifs and strays and sent by some charitable organisation to do farmwork in Australia.

The first Reuben ever knew was a letter that came two years after the boys had left home. "Just a few words hoping you are well as it leaves us the same," it said.

18

Emily continued to mother the little ones until she left school and entered domestic service locally. When she was 19 she came home to bear a child and with only her mother in attendance, forced herself to stifle her groans lest the neighbours should hear. Then, in the dark hours, she too, escaped, carrying her baby. She went by the short cut, stumbling over the gravestones of the churchyard and running through the wet grass of the paddock. From that day not a word, good or ill, was heard of Emily again.

I do not know what other blows there were for Reuben from the cruel conditions at the end of the century but remembering how completely alone he was in his old age it seems probable that there were others of the family who took the short cut away from the cottage and the village.

The facts could be pieced together from the records but I have already pried too much. Not all that is the substance of daily life is ever recorded and there must have been events and days of cheer and contentment whose passing would not merit a mention in the Family Bible, but whose memory could have helped to sustain the old man as he sat and waited in his chair.

Pigs for Market

The Pratt family were up betimes. Fred Pratt himself had already gone across to the buildings long before daylight. When young Joe came down he found his mother in the kitchen, not yet properly dressed, making tea beside the flaring stove.

"Yew better git out there an' lend a hand, Joe," she said anxiously. "Come back for breakfast later on. Tha's somethin' about the pigs -"

"What about the pigs?" Joe wanted to know.

"I don't know - but he's to git 'em away quick. He ain't stopped to have bite or sup yit."

Joe came out of the kitchen into the fresh morning air and pulled his jacket closer as he crossed to the pigsties. His father and old Dobbler were already there with a lantern that guttered in the breeze.

Despite the cool wind, Fred Pratt was working as usual in his shirtsleeves hurriedly fixing up hurdles outside the pig gate. He was driving in stakes while Dobbler, the pensioner, held the hurdles upright.

Dobbler had long ago rejected the need to hurry and fret, and from time to time he essayed remarks which he hoped would detract Fred from his frantic haste and lead to a more conversational and philosophic view of the situation.

Fred, however, was in no such mood. As soon as Joe came up, he said, "Yew git the hoss riddy, Joe, sune as yew can. Don't stop for nothen - feed him later on. Git him in the cart."

"What - are yew a-takin' the pigs, 'en?" asked Joe, but his father had disappeared into the darkness to find boards to make a ramp to the back of the cart. The hurdles were already in place, making a short corridor from the pig pen gate and Dobbler stayed to sprinkle some straw along.

He took unkindly to such unseemly haste and when he had finished his task he walked across to the stable to have a word with Joe and to light his pipe in peace.

"That on't ever dew ter hurry pigs," he pronounced. "Pigs is somethin' yew atter take time over. Sune as there's any fuss, they git suspicious an' they balk. Them blarm grut sows in that sty - no one will ever git them to go one way dew they want to go the t'other."

Joe wondered, too, as he hurriedly prepared the horse, what all the urgency was about.

"I reckon I know why," said Dobbler ruminatively. "That don't take a lot o' workin' out, arter all. They got swine fever or somp'n over at Larksgreen. Sune as they know sartain sure tha's catchin', they'll hev a order stoppin' all pigs bein' moved. Yew know what that'd mean to yer father better'n what I dew."

Joe did know. In the meagre returns of the smallholding, the sale of pigs was of utmost importance. Fattened and taken to market twice a year, they filled the gaps between the cash crops of potatoes and early rhubarb and were necessary to the basic income of the family.

The six huge baconers in the sty were due to go to market and their going was imperative.

It was already lighter when he brought the horse

21

out and harnessed it to the cart. At the back of the cart the ramp was in place; it was steep. They'll never get up that ramp, Joe thought.

The pigs were beginning to squeal now, clamouring for their breakfast. Joe took a stick and climbed over the gate into the seething, shrieking mob while Dobbler took up his post by the gate.

Fred Pratt threw the old pig net over the cart and wondered whether the frail hurdles and the ramp would hold against the uncertain temper of old sows. But there was no time for more.

"One at a time," he shouted.

Dobbler opened the gate and Joe drove out the first of the pigs. Despite the straw it was immediately suspicious, took a dislike to old Dobbler standing there and turned in a panic to the world it knew.

"Let it go back," shouted Fred; "Try another." The next pig emerged peacably enough, saw something edible and trotted along the run with Fred urging it from behind. At the ramp it jibbed but found it could not go back and escaped both evils at once by pushing its snout under a hurdle and pushing free.

Fred was cursing and sweating, unsure whether to chase after the sow but Dobbler was shouting: "Another one a-comin'."

"Keep 'em back, yew silly owd-" but the remaining pigs suddenly decided they would keep together, pushed through the gate in a stampede, discovered the weakness of the hurdles and all disappeared into the field. After the shrieking and shouting it was suddenly quiet.

"We on't git 'em back - not without help," said

Joe. His father was leaning against the cart, breathless and tired, but desperate to get the pigs sold.

"There's on'y one thing left," he decided, "an' that'll be up to yew, Joe. They'll drive out o' the field easy enough through the bottom gate on to the rood. Yew'll atter drive 'em all the way."

Joe said nothing, but Dobbler was shaking his head until he saw the look of desperation on Fred Pratt's face, then he said: "Yew want me to go tew?"

"That'd be a help. Yew'll atter git 'em there afore mid-day. Ask for Arthur Brundle - don't hev any truck wi' anybody else."

Joe and Dobbler drove the pigs out on to the road in a miserable despair of ever getting them to market. They began prodding and shouting, heading them off from gateways, from turning back, trying to keep them moving. It was cruel, Joe thought. their mobility had been bred out of them. It was cruel to force them along.

Conditions became worse as the sun came up, beating strong and bright on the pigs' backs. At mid-morning all six went down one after another, laying their gross weight against the ground as if they would never get up. It took 20 minutes to get them on their feet again and now they were twice as bad tempered and obstinate.

Old Dobbler too, was showing that the walk was too much for him. When they reached a handy pub at the side of the road, Joe persuaded him to stay there and let him finish the journey on his own.

Half a mile from the market the pigs went down again, grunting and panting in the gutter and in the shade of the trees.

On his own Joe found it impossible to get them up again. In a kind of inspired desperation he ran to the back of a nearby cottage and asked for a can of water. It was the only thing he could think of and perhaps the only thing that would have done any good.

He sprayed the huge bodies with ice-cold water from the cottage well and they twitched and shook and stood up. At last, at half-past eleven the pigs flopped into the market place and into one of the many empty pens.

Joe wiped his face and looked around. The market was almost empty and everywhere were posters and notices that proclaimed that as from nine o'clock that morning it was unlawful to move pigs from their quarters.

A handful of officials, including a policeman, gathered round Joe and the pen. It seemed they were not unwilling to accept the pigs but were considering a breach of the law.

"We didn't know about no Order afore we started out," protested Joe. "We was on the road afore nine o'clock."

It seemed to change the situation. The officials consulted together and agreed that the Order could not have been contravened; moreover, it would do more harm than good to move the animals again. They were included as pigs which had arrived before the Order could be enforced.

Joe sat on some straw in an empty pen until the market closed, then claimed the cheque and set off home.

He wanted to feel pleased, triumphant, that all had

turned out well in the end, to recount his adventures to his mother and father. But when he got home and found his father sitting clean and dignified but tired at the kitchen table and his mother waiting with food for him, he knew there was no triumph.

In the quiet he ate his food and shared with them the unspoken hazards of the day, the fatigue from the endless fighting, the sense of meanness at having to circumvent authority, and the overwhelming suspicion that all he had gained from ill-fortune was a temporary respite.

Percy's Stand

Like many another Suffolk village, that in which I spent some part of my childhood used to be so unassuming that its charms were scarcely ever noticed.

It still stands in comparative peace a half-mile from a busy turnpike and in practical terms it has not changed very much.

The expanse of The Green is still there and round about it are the farms, the cottages we knew as the Row and the small school.

Now the school is empty and grass grows through the tarmac of the playground and hides the splinters of glass broken from half-a-dozen panes in the tall, forlorn-looking windows. Apart from this it is difficult to say that anything has changed, though even as one admits it there comes the feeling that in fact nothing is the same.

In the last few decades a superficial metamorphosis has taken place in which once-unconsidered charms have been prettied up and the bucolic face of the village has become prim and proper to face a different world.

Look at The Green for example. As I remember it, long before it became tamed and titivated by Best-Kept-Village mentality, The Green was a rare piece of wild, common waste.

It had a couple of ponds fringed with bramble and blackthorn where coot and water-rat could live in tolerable peace when boys were not fishing.

Skylarks used to sing high up over the drifts of dog-daisies and waist-high buttercups; a partridge regularly reared its young from the nest on the edge of a hollow pitted with rabbit burrows.

Now all such vulgarities have gone - the very primness of The Green would repulse wild life even if it had not been destroyed already by poison sprays, myxomatosis and the like.

At least, they say, The Green is tidy. Tidy, too, is the churchyard which has been razed and reduced to something of complete insignificance and all of it for the convenience of the motor mower. The hedge banks have been tidied with weed-killer and leaves have been tidied by cutting down trees.

What has been lost? Nothing that can be calculated. All that has gone is the nebulous quality of undisciplined nature - so rich and effulgent once that it flowed and flooded in great waves of insect-humming odour into the homes and lives of country people.

It was this that escaped some time during the tidying-up, an essence that disappeared so quietly that no one could say exactly when it happened and so completely that no one could ever expect to know it again.

In earlier days there used to be no road at all on the side of The Green where the school stands, and only a broken fence to distinguish the playground.

Children poured out of school into the heath and broom that grew in the sandy soil on that side and made their way across The Green by tracks as much frequented by wild creatures as by humans.

27

Many of the children made for the Row where the large families lived, and in no time at all were back on The Green with thick slices of bread and jam or bread and dripping.

Some of the families of the Row were rough; in those earlier days of compulsory schooling they took unkindly to the notion of sending children to school.

Nevertheless, as time went on both village and school could well have contrived to live together but for one thing - the bugbear of the annual school inspection.

From this everyone suffered - school, teachers, parents, and most of all, pupils, for it was upon the individual child's standard and attendance that the grant to the school was based. Yet little was done in the way of protest until Percy Bower made his desperate stand on August 5th, 1894.

On that fine, summer morning the Inspector had arrived, checked the register and set about examining the children in the pedantic manner of that time.

When Percy Bower came to stand before him, the Inspector was making a great to-do about the pronounciation of a word.

Percy Bower stood dumbly, sinking from sheer fright into sullen defiance.

As the hated voice went on and on, Percy raised one foot and glowered at the inspectorial waistcoat button nearest to him until the limit came and the metal-capped boot shot forward with the viciousness of panic.

It brought a sharp "oh" from the enemy as the boot landed on his shin.

Then, as if to emphasise that his previous actions

were by no means to be construed as friendly, he spat in the direction of the waistcoat buttons and was off like an eel past the hands that tried to detain him.

From this time Percy was to have a largely undeserved reputation as a scamp and a rebel. The truth was that his wrong-doings, as in this instance, were usually negative and extricative.

When his poor comprehension placed him in a situation that was untenable he felt sullen and defeated and had to fight to free himself. He hid himself on The Green for the rest of that day, playing hide-and-seek with the School Board man who succeeded in getting his feet very wet in rashly following Percy over the stepping stones across the larger pond. In the evening Percy was still at large but close-harried by the minions of authority. Next day he turned up at school as usual.

It was about this time that educationists began to relent a little over the teaching of the three 'Rs'. From now on the curriculum would become more liberal with the introduction of subjects like needle-work and singing. So enchanted were head teachers over this relaxation that new achievements were recorded - sometimes in very odd contexts - in the school log book.

Only a few weeks before, the head mistress of this small school had written:

"Sixteen boys are away stone-picking in the fields. Learned a new hymn tune - Hold the Fort."

On the day that Percy returned in disgrace, taking his six strokes of the cane and a long evening detention, the headmistress was recording the day's highlights in her own words: "Taught the children a new hymn tune - Now the Day is Over. Kept Percy Bower in until eight o' clock for bad conduct."

Poor Percy; the day was slow to be over for him. As he stood on a form and looked out of the window on to the endless life of The Green, it must have seemed that a lifetime had passed him by.

A whole summer's evening had been taken from his life and in harvest time, too.

I wonder if Percy ever forgot that hymn!

Tuffy Dean

The parish records that deal with "Tuffy" Dean are scant but illuminating: at his death only "Old Dean." Neither he nor anyone else knew his Christian name for certain and the epithet covered the omission very suitably for it was as Old Dean or Tuffy that he was generally known in his adopted village.

Nothing at all is recorded for him among the marriages though the clerk's pen must have been ink-dipped and ready on many occasions for in earlier years he was a man much favoured by the village servant girls.

As for his birth, it was not until later that searches revealed him to be Frederick and "base-born" as indicated by the endorsement in the margin of the register.

Even his nickname was not at all certain, for those who could remember his arrival in the village, "from nowhere" (actually from the neighbouring county of Essex, which was much the same thing to the local people) could recollect that it was originally Diddecoy, and this too was illuminating. However, it was as Tuffy that he became known and eventually accepted though he was always qualified as a "rum bloke" in private conversation.

It was Tuffy's immense capacity for work that caused wonder and created legend. In himself he was never a forthcoming character - his mind looked inwards with some kind of shouldering-off of the

31

world about him, an impatient dissatisfaction that was strange to his humbler fellow workers. As he grew older his introspection grew deeper and his path lonelier, and women who would have dared a man's anger were chary of his brooding resentment.

His relief came only in his passion for work, for he attacked whatever farm task came to hand with a kind of nervous violence that "whooly stammed" the natives and delighted the farmer who employed him. In time he became head man at the farm and would have been the Lord of the Harvest but for the innovation of the mechanical reapers.

As it was he had often led a team of 15 men into the harvest field, - and quickly left them behind as he cut the first swathe with his scythe, "as fast," it was said, "as a man could walk". But the new reaping machines were already clacking and taking the corn away from the scythes, and as the clacking grew so the mowing team dwindled to mere clearers of the headlands for the convenience of the machine.

Part of Tuffy's enthusiasm for work lay in the particular care and pride that he took in his tools. His cutting tools were of the finest that cunning and experience could make, his scythe light and handy with a slim, smooth-grained stale that was the envy of lesser men. "Why, tha's on'y a doddy little thing" they would say, comparing it with their own heavier scythes and he would answer shortly: "Lighter the timber, better the blade," and prove it with the speed of his work. His accomplished mowing was a lesson to all, for the scythe was no easy tool for the beginner to master, and many a one who could only "cut some, cover some and dozzle some" (dozzle means to stun or stupefy) learned the secret at his hands.

However, it seemed that the day of the mower and the hand-worker generally was coming to an end. It was something that shocked the farm men and drove Tuffy to despair; the day of his personal dominance in the field was over. The time came when in desperation he sought to prove to the farmer that he could equal the achievement of the clacking machine by his own strength and speed with a scythe and nothing would satisfy him but a proper trial in the cornfield.

It was a contest so unequal that the conclusion must have been easily foreseen by all except Tuffy. The reaping machine, pulled by two round-bellied Punchs, was to have a handicap of ten yards and the race limited to one swathe across the field.

On a fine morning in early September, Tuffy advanced ten yards into a bay in the cornfield, his sharpened and polished scythe ready, and at the signal, set to furiously to the task. Perhaps no one had ever mowed at that speed before, but it was not quick enough for the mechanical reaper. As the hated sound grew nearer Tuffy worked in a frenzy until the horses drew level and then overtook.

Suddenly, in the same movement as he cut through the corn, he threw the scythe sideways at the machine. It was a gesture of despair and anger that renounced all that he had believed in and worked for. No one could have foreseen the tragic consequences. The precious scythe landed on the cutters and was disintegrated into a hundred flying missiles, one of which gashed Tuffy's leg. Other pieces struck the horses which immediately bolted with the rocking machine and the frightened driver still behind them. Only the ditch stopped the runaways and there the sad reckoning was made of one horse killed and a man with a broken collar-bone.

Tuffy was sacked on the spot and his cottage ordered to be vacated within a week. During the same evening what seemed to be the whole village population gathered outside his door making "rough music" on tin pans and kettles to drive him away. Go he would have done if he had known any place to go.

In the end a shoemaker living on the edge of the village took him in and taught him the trade. Tuffy transferred his zest for workmanship to the new skills and lived there for the next 15 years, quietly and half-forgotten, until his sight failed. On the same day that he gave up his tools he took his own life, using the old shotgun that his employer used for shooting rabbits.

Frankie and George

I n the slow, cold waking of an October morning in 1910, a light appeared dimly in the cowman's room above the nettice on Dowson's Farm and another in the bedroom of the farmhouse. The day — a day that two small boys would remember for the rest of their lives — had inauspiciously begun.

The farmyard was still dark with shadows when the cowman, Walter Brett, came down with the lantern and busied himself with the cows. In a little while the farmer appeared and gave a hand with the milking.

The men's movements were shadowed large and slow on the whitewashed walls beside the complaisant cows and seemed to be part of the lethargy of the morning. When the farmer had milked two cows he took a turnip watch from his waistcoat pocket and held it close to the lantern, but the dim light defeated his poor eyesight and he took the watch to show to Walter.

"What dew that say?" he asked.

"That say half arter seven - tha's what that say," the cowman replied, ill-temperedly. "That 'ere boy should 'a bin heah a half arr ago. I don't reckon he's any blessed use to anybody."

"Ah, tha's a funny family," mused the farmer. "They're a proper rum owd lot - don't b'long round here. Come from away somewhere."

"Oh, ah," said Walter, as if this explained everything.

"Yew see what he say when he git here," advised the farmer, going off to the farmhouse for his breakfast. "But don't stand any owd buck. We can manage athout what little work he dew."

At about that moment two small figures were advancing along the shadowy road from the village, their feet crunching anxiously on the gritty surface as they hurried to make up time. One was the absentee, 12-year-old Frankie Biggs, and the other his younger brother George.

George was still a pupil at the village school but was committed to accompanying his brother on every possible occasion by his unswerving affection, strong enough to bring him from his bed on any morning.

When they reached the church the clock showed an unbelievable quarter to eight.

Frankie gasped. "Walter 'ont half be roiled," he said.

"Yew cou'n't help that," said George loyally. "But 'haps that'd be better not to go at all. That'll be eight o'clock afore yew git there. Owd Walter - he'll jest about kill yew."

They stopped in despair beside the signpost at the end of the farm lane. It only added to their panic when they climbed the bank and could see the lights glimmering at the farm.

Frankie said gloomily: "Ef I git the sack I dussent go hoom."

George looked at his brother hopefully. "We could run away," he said. "We could both on us run away togither."

For a minute they looked at each other. Then Frankie said: "Yew wait heah till huppast eight, then yew better git to school. Ef they gi' me the sack I'll be back afore then. I got to go to git my wages."

George played in the lane beside the signpost while the day rose afresh and showed its cheerful, mellow autumn face. He wanted so much to do new and daring things with Frankie, and would have waited all day if need be.

When Frankie appeared just before half past eight with a scarlet ear and tears on his eyelashes - but a shilling in his pocket - they turned their backs on Dowson's Farm and ran off into the sun.

Although they had talked of running away, the serious matter of travelling a distance was immediately forgotten. It was adventure and freedom, lightness of heart, that they sought; all else, the gloomy thoughts of punishment and retribution were driven by excitement and the warm sun into the back of their minds.

At the village shop they bought a packet of Wild Woodbine cigarettes, a box of matches and half a loaf of bread. They still had sixpence left. In high spirits they entered fields, shinned up trees, followed tracks and plunged through woods.

Then, on the very edge of the village, beside what must once have been the village green, they found everything that they were looking for. There was a great deal of unwanted space, a small flowing creek with watercress growing, old derelict buildings and an empty windmill. There was also a hollow tree.

"We could a'most live in there," said George.

They managed to squeeze into the rotten centre of the old tree and lit their secret cigarettes with hilarious ceremony, but soon tired of the business and got out of the stump to explore the creek, paddling well up-stream until another farmhouse came into view.

When they came back they found that the cigarettes they had rejected inside the hollow stump had ignited some dead material and the trunk was belching smoke. It seemed of no importance. Their great excitement lay in the deserted windmill.

"Tha's jest like a castle keep," said George. "No one could ever git in there ef yew din't want 'em tew."

They ate up the bread and spent the whole of the long, mellow afternoon in the mill, fighting for good or evil causes, attacking and defending, building defences and fashioning weapons. It was not until five o'clock that George looked out of the narrow mill window and saw that his castle was indeed besieged.

Something like half a dozen recognisable characters, all on the side of gloomy adult rectitude, were advancing across the open space towards the mill. The boys stared; all of a sudden the sun had gone.

In a sober review of their activities they could see how the chain of retribution had begun and developed throughout the day.

First, George's absence from school yet again had caused the irate teacher to demand an explanation from the parents. Their father had stormed to the school and the School Board man had been sent for.

Then their father had stormed along to Dowson's Farm and found that Frankie had gone too and had used insulting language to Walter Brett.

All of these individuals, in addition to the village constable when they discovered the crowning anarchy

38

of the smouldering stump, followed the wanton trail to the old mill.

Suddenly the boys saw that the world was their enemy. George pushed his brother to a rear exit.

"Yew better clear out, Frankie. They can't send me to a reformatory but they can yew. Yew git away while I keep 'em busy."

He stopped to watch Frankie go. "Cheerio, Frankie," he said. Then for half an hour he rained missiles on to the astonished people below, shouting insults and shooting arrows until a whole crowd of villagers had gathered. Then, suddenly he became quiet and came down. Frankie would be clear away and George knew in his heart that he would never see him again.

Because of his frequent absences from school and this latest escapade, George was sent to a truant school for six weeks and suffered the harsh discipline there. When he came home he seemed forever lost without his brother.

As for Frankie, he fled from the village and from all knowledge. It was not until the 1914-18 War that George received a letter from Frankie urging him to go out and join him in Australia. But George was needed to fight and in 1916 he joined the thousands of the doomed upon the Somme, to die without the glory of a castle to defend or a brother to love.

Many years later Frankie came with his Australian family to visit the village. Alone, he walked the lanes to the farm and the old mill, looking and listening, as if he could still see and hear George defending his castle and shrilling the cause of freedom.

"It was a wonderful day," he told his wife. "The

39

best day of my life - the only day we really had together. I shall never know what we did that was so wrong."

Grandma

You must have seen the hut where the Upsons used to live. Of course, it doesn't look so much like a hut now - face-lifting attentions over the years have allowed it to merge into the general ugliness of the encroaching housing estate - but underneath there is still the original shell of corrugated iron and at the ends the bullet-pocked walls that the Upsons knew.

The first winter that the Upsons moved into their newly-made home soon after the 1914-18 War was one that Peter Upson remembered to the end of his life. It had been snowing, he recalled, and the younger boys of the family crammed the snow into saucepans to make a dull, black liquid that was a trifle better than the strong taste of pond water, though in the dry summer that followed even the pond water became precious.

Peter was one of the youngest of the extensive Upson family. He had been eight years old in the December in which the family moved into the hut and could dimly remember something of the activity and excitement if the time.

When he was old enough to realise the extent of his family's achievement it was always a surprise to recall the flavour of enjoyment and freedom of that first winter, rough and cold though it was, and of the hot summer that followed and the years after.

During the war, the two-acre field and the long, timber hut had been occupied by soldiers. The hut itself was a rifle range for recruits, and consisted of a mere shell with an earth floor.

At one end was a trench dug into the earth from which rifles were fired at the blank, brick wall at the other. It was one of Peter's first jobs to pick up the spent bullets out of the dry earth, and outside in the field, to pile up some of the debris left by the army.

His father and older brothers were occupied with more urgent work - no less than the conversion of the hut into a place for the family to live.

Somehow, the long hut was split into two - one end to provide sheds and outbuildings, the other for the dwelling house. Floors and ceilings were added to the living quarters, windows and board partitions to form separate rooms.

As soon as the place was weather-proof and basically habitable, the family began moving their possessions from the cottage where they had lived about a mile off.

The moving was a simple, if repetitive operation. Everything was ferried along the lanes on a small handcart and there were always several willing, small hands to keep the load balanced and moving.

It was a task given to the lesser members of the family, who were desperately exerted sometimes by the difficulties of the conveyance. The trouble was that, with only two wheels and no legs, it was liable to tip up at the slightest unbalance and deposit its load into the road.

Peter remembered afterwards how particularly awkward the mangle had been to manoeuvre and how, when at last it was dumped outside the door of the hut, it stood there for weeks like some indignant washerwoman waiting for permission to enter.

On the last day before the family moved in, the handcart was trundled back and forwards without rest and any youngsters not actually pushing the cart had to carry bundles of goods in their arms. By teatime there was a chaos of things in and around the half-finished home and a hurried concern for the priorities of bedding and food.

In the evening, Fred, the eldest son, took the horse and cart and fetched the pigs and chickens. At last, everything had been carried along to the new dwelling - except for grandmother.

Grandmother Upson had been left to the last for the simple reason that she was the most difficult to budge. She sat to the last in her cane chair in the middle of the kitchen floor as forbidding as Canute of the tide of change. For several days she had moved little, ate grudgingly, and maintained a martyred. silence. In answer to the most placatory persuasion by the rest of the family she would retort waspishly:

"I ain't a-goin', cos this is my hoom. That there place 'on't ever be hoom to me. But o' course haps tha's a good thing gittin' me driv out o' me own hoom cos I shan't last long 'en: I shan't be no burden to no one 'en."

When it was clear that persuasion was useless, the family picked up Grandma and her chair together and placed them in the handcart. She sat there all the way along the lanes as brooding and sour-faced as if she were going to the gallows.

At the hut she consented to get down and survey the raw, unpainted rooms and the unwelcoming concrete floor of the kitchen.

The sheer chaos of moving a large family into such conditions seemed to stir her sensibilities. She began to perk up immediately, rejected the chair and applied herself to the practical difficulties in front of her.

From then on, Grandma was a tower of strength and ingenuity that kept the family going during the hard times, using for her guide her own hard experiences of the past.

The day after the family moved in, Fred managed to shoot a pheasant over the hedge. Shooting thus over the hedge into adjoining fields considerably enlarged the two acres belonging to the hut so far as game was concerned; the difficulty, sometimes, was to retrieve the victim without being seen.

In this case the deed had been done soon after daylight and the body quickly recovered. Fred's triumph would have been complete if he could have found a way of roasting the pheasant since there was no oven in the hut and he spent some time optimistically beating out some old biscuit tins to line an improvised kiln in the open field.

Unfortunately, the techniques of oven lore defeated him, and in the end the pheasant was put like everything else into the big, black pot over the open fire in the hut.

It was this pot that forever provided its offerings of smoke-flavoured food to the family. Grandma took over this primitive cooking arrangement and somehow could always be depended on to ladle out good broth and dumplings, rabbit stew and vegetables. No one was ever hungry for long.

How was it, Peter wondered afterwards, how was it

that we were so happy? Was it because we were young and knew no better or because it was a kind of adventure, or because you could live as you liked without the bureaucratic interference?

Perhaps, he thought, a bit of all these things. Putting up with hardship is not difficult provided you have your freedom. Anyway, it was not the food nor the discomfort that proved the major problem during those first few months, but much more the lack of water.

Early on in the project the expectation of sinking their own well had had to be rejected by the Upsons because of the expense of digging to the depth required.

Unfortunately the drought of that first year increased the needs of the family and stock, while the level of the pond dropped lower and lower, until Grandma declared the remaining sludge unsuitable for anything.

Instead, she ordered two galvanised rubbish bins from the ironmongers and indicated that they must be kept filled with water - somehow. At the same time she placed beside the rainwater butts a series of tubs and containers of diminishing size so that any overflow would be saved.

Water supplies for the bins were not difficult while Fred could fetch it from the spring in the next village. As the dry period went on, however, even this began to decrease.

The local villagers, concerned for their own supplies, waited for Fred at his next visit and drove him off.

For a time the supply was piecemeal. Any one of

the family who went to a pub, a shop, visited a neighbour or a girl-friend carried with him, as a matter of course, a couple of bottles for water.

In the end, rain came with cloud bursts that thundered down on the corrugated roof and poured musically into the waiting containers. Peter could remember standing in the rain, looking and listening as if it were a personal beneficence.

Is this what we have lost, he wondered, the commerce with the necessary things, the fight for basic needs? Was it this that made those days so exciting and absorbing - so that at last even Grandma had to declare the hut was "hoom, sweet hoom"?

Old Ben

Early in the morning old Ben shuffled across the farmyard carrying his half-filled egg-pail from the dairy. At the five-barred gate he stumbled slightly in the ridges of mud and clattered his pail against the post.

In a moment Simon the stockman was calling from the mixing shed. "Hoyd up, you owd fule. Y'u'll hev them eggs upset one o' these days."

He stood in the rectangle of light in the doorway, handbowl full of oats, waiting cheerfully for a reply. But Ben was silent for the time it took to unhook the chain, enter the paddock and shut the gate again.

"Ef I dew," he said finally, "I 'on't ask you to pick 'em up." Off he went, chuckling at the customary exchange of wit, to tread a curving diagonal of footprints in the dew of the paddock as he made for his cottage and the off-hand farm.

Old Ben was 70. In his heyday he had been the head horseman and a man of consequence. Now, having seen the last of the horses go and the old times with them, Ben looked after the hens. It was something that kept him occupied for a few hours a day and brought him up to the home farm before day-break every morning like an old horse broken to a routine that it could not change.

Half-way across the paddock Ben thought of another rejoinder that he could have made and immediately came to a halt and looked back at the farm buildings as if inclined to deliver the bon mot forthwith.

There was still a pale light at the mixing shed door and another in the farmhouse where the family would be coming downstairs. From the dark huddle of buildings that still seemed asleep there came a subdued stirring, with the occasional blare of a calf and the clatter of a pail, while in the pigsties already a slowly rising pitch of noise welcomed the daybreak and the smell of food.

Having collected the eggs from the home farm, it was Ben's duty to continue his poultry chores at the implement sheds flatteringly called the off-hand farm. Here, in the manner of an earlier type of farming a couple of score of fowls survived, living as they could and laying where they wished.

It was a pleasant, nostalgic task for Ben to search the buildings and the stackyard for nests and to take his special basket to gather the eggs. On Fridays the egg van came and collected one filled box and left another.

Early next morning, Ben walked down to the home farm again, picked up his pail and went past the mixing shed to the gate. Simon was filling his buckets at the stand-pipe.

"Wotcher, Ben," he called. "Yew got yar eggs then." He came through the gloom and looked into the pail. "Cor-blast - the way yew stagger about with that pail, I thought that was full. There ain't more'n a couple of dozen. Yew mind yew don't injure yourself."

"Ah," returned Ben equably, "don't yew forgit me imfirmity." He held up his arm which had become twisted years before when a plough horse had bolted.

For a moment he felt he had kept up his end of the conversation for Simon disappeared clattering into the mixing shed. Then he came to the door again and watched Ben stumble along towards the gate. "Yo're a imfirm owd bastard," he shouted in his loud, insensitive way. Ben grinned, but could think of nothing else to say.

A couple of days later, Simon was shouting across the yard; "I forgot yo're a hossman. You orter a' brought a hoss to help yew carry them eggs."

Ben walked on, hoping he hadn't heard anything about horses. "A coupla hosses an' a wagon - yew could git them eggs away without any trouble." Ben could think of nothing to say.

Back at the off-hand place, Ben brought out his box seat covered in an old meal sack and stretched out in the thin October sun. Simon's remarks had never irked him until now and deep down he knew it was because of the way Simon had spoken of horses.

It was a subject of Ben's experience so special and personal that he could not hear the taunt without a thumping at his heart. In the hours of his meditation and in his dreams the world was one where there were horses still.

The next morning Ben walked quietly on the ridges of mud in the yard and escaped the badinage. But he met Simon on the following morning coming out of the paddock with a handkerchief full of mushrooms.

"I reckon tha's one good thing about hosses," he said. "They make the mushrooms grow."

Ben tried to think of something that would make them laugh but he couldn't. Instead he found himself saying in a low voice: "You don't know anything about horses do you?"

"No," answered Simon promptly. "Nor want to, neether."

"Well, they got more sense 'n tractors, 'an tractor drivers too - some on 'em."

"Don't you believe it. Ef hosses had any sense they wou'n't dew what they dew dew, they're bloody well big enough."

Ben went off home. In the afternoon he walked over to Patterson's farm a mile away where the last Suffolk Punch in the neighbourhood had been retired to grass.

The foreman, knowing Ben's reputation with horses, had no hesitation in allowing him to take it for a few days' feed and exercise.

Simon looked out of his mixing shed in astonishment the next morning when he heard the great horse entering the yard. In the half light the Punch looked unbelievably huge and powerful and Ben a figure of majesty.

"Dew yew git outa the way," said Ben from his lofty perch. "He eat little men like yew for breakfast."

But surprise and curiosity kept Simon in close proximity, and when Ben slipped off the great broad back, nothing would suit Simon but to mount the stallion himself. "You want to sit well back," said Ben cruelly. Then in a moment he had given the horse a sharp smack on the rump and shouted loud and clear: "Home ye go."

The great stallion shook itself and turned, headed for the gate and was off down the road at an energetic walk with Simon clinging to its rump.

Unfamiliarity with horses and moving hoofs kept him nervously mounted for the distance of a quarter of a mile before he found the nerve to slide off. It was long enough.

Two of the farm men saw, so did Mrs. Dewes who saw everything; so did the boss's wife, drawn to the window by the unaccustomed sound of hoofs.

When Simon, bruised and shaken, got back to the yard, the boss was there.

"That's a rum time o' the day to go hoss riding," he said.

The two farm men hovered nearby. "I reckon he's training for one o' them gymkhanas," one said loudly.

"More like a circus rider, I reckon," said the other.

Ben felt no need to walk quietly in the yard the next morning. He poked his head into the mixing shed door.

"Tha's a rare morning for a ride. Where shall you go this morning?"

There was no answer. Ben went off chuckling to himself.

He could think of enough witty remarks to keep Simon quiet for months.

Adam and the victoria

The corn stood fresh green and then golden
yellow: but it stood and became amber-coloured
and dark before ever the reaping began. The rain
drove into the wheat and the farm men waited and
watched and saw the ears blacken with age and
disease.

They saw the rain over and over again, and could
feel through their drooping spirits how the grain that
should have made bread was shedding on to the wet
ground.

It was shedding and bursting into another abortive
life-cycle with long white roots sometimes even before it left the ear. When it was too late the sun came
again, and the farmers sent their self-binders into the
fields to cut and destroy the ugly black straw.

The men were silent. There was nothing more to be
said about the rain, but there was nothing more
worth saying about anything else either, for without
the harvest nothing was important. They were surly
with each other and the farmer was even more surly
than they, for his disappointment was superior to
theirs.

On Meadowsfield Farm the men set about carting
the manure from the yards without much heart. In
other years this had been a cheerful job that followed
the triumphant climax of the harvest: the beginning
of a new year.

Now it was a sour experience to start again when

the whole of the previous year's work had been washed out by the rain.

In the corners of the fields some of the straw still stood and showed the odd flash of a scarlet poppy or yellow charlock. Here one or two of the women sought unavailingly for ears that had not germinated.

The men saw the women there, their own wives, and turned away and said nothing.

When they came to Pond Field, out of sight of the farmhouse, the men rested at last, leaning on their cromes beside the steaming heaps of manure that they had pulled from the tumbrils. Old Fred, who was the oldest man on the farm, walked round to the lee of the horse to fill his pipe with loose shag and light it.

"That stand to reason," he said mildly, knowing what the others were thinking, "that stand to reason he 'on't keep all on us through the winter. He 'a' got a hull year to wait afore he git any more money comin' in. Dew yew see, he'll be a'cuttin' down on min afore long." Adam nodded, but Barney, with a young wife and five children, was sullen and defensive.

"I lay his belly 'on't suffer much in cowd weather. What about all the money he got salted away from other harvests? They ain't all failed."

Adam was sorry for him, and for the other men who had large families waiting at home. For himself, he regretted the bad harvest and the prospect of a lean winter but it would not kill him: nor would it harm Elsie, his wife, for they had no family to consider.

Moreover, if it came to it, he could sell the victoria.

53

Whenever he thought of the victoria he could not help smiling. It was an absurd thing to possess, something that rightly belonged to the gentry class, yet it was his and perhaps he would sell it to make up for the harvest money.

Of course, it would be difficult for Elsie. To her - much more than to him - the victoria had become a possession of pride - a symbol of an elegance that might otherwise never be known to her. She would not like it to go - static, impotent thing though it was (for they would never have horse to pull it) and perhaps it would never come to the point of necessity.

Adam's uncle had been given the carriage by a go-ahead squire who was enamoured of the new-fangled motor cars and needed the space in his coach-house. The uncle had no space either and lodged it at Adam's in the big shed he had built to house his cagebirds.

When the uncle died there was neither will nor relatives beyond Adam and there was nothing else to do but to keep it. Adam regarded the unusual acquisition with mixed feelings, often thinking of all the cages of birds that the shed might have housed - but Elsie was obsessed with her ownership.

On summer evenings she would sit in the garden on the little needlework chair and watch as Adam drew the carriage out of the shed and cleaned it once again though dirt and dust had barely had time to accumulate. She never tired of admiring the delicate lines and the fragile elegance that nothing else that they owned possessed. It set her slightly apart from the village folk and hinted at a knowledge of genteel living. To

Elsie the victoria was of the very sweetness of life.

In November, two of the men were sacked from Meadowsfield Farm: it was believed there would soon be others. The older men shook off their careful ways and worked beside the younger men and struggled to keep up.

Every man tried to show himself to be indispensable - but collectively they only hastened the day of reckoning through doing prodigies of work. After Christmas two more of the men left and joined those discarded from other farms.

In the village the cottages were silent; already four whole families had been taken to the workhouse. Men spoke desperately of going to work in the towns but no one knew how to set about it. Instead, they prepared themselves as best they could for the months ahead.

"We may have to sell the victoria," Adam told Elsie. Her mouth opened for a moment with the shock, then her face became sullen, though what she was thinking she kept to herself.

Perhaps I can hold on for a time, Adam thought. But January came mercilessly into their home and into the defenceless homes of the villagers. Cold, rather than hunger, became the arch enemy, especially of the older folk.

On the same day that he learned that old Fred was without a fire, Adam took the victoria from the shed, almost hating its bright, trim superiority and hauled it along the lane to the woods. Barney helped him load and cart the sere timber to Fred's door and to the doors of the old people. Then the snow came and they could not push the victoria.

When Fred had used all the timber Adam said that he would break up the victoria for fuel but the old man would not allow it. A little later, the victoria was used instead to carry the old man's body to the cemetery to save the cost of a hearse.

Elsie watched and saw how the victoria was becoming battered and broken and for this more than anything else she became despondent.

When Adam urged her to spend the rest of the winter with her relatives in the town, she was ready to agree. He was relieved to think that she would be cared for. It was a sensible thing to do. But in his heart he knew that she had gone because he had destroyed the beauty of the victoria.

Alone, Adam fought the winter for himself and for his friends. When the spring came and the village began to stir again, the victoria was a sorry sight, though still surprisingly whole.

It stood, no longer cared for, while the summer months led on to harvest once again.

Once again the corn became yellow, and there was no rain. The corn stood and was harvested and women followed into the fields and gleaned all that they needed for the winter flour.

Then, at last, Elsie wrote. Adam sat in his cottage and placed the letter unopened on the mantelpiece.

After the harvest was over he hauled the victoria for the last time out of the yard and on to the waste land. There he filled it and covered it with the fresh golden straw from the fields and set Elsie's needlework chair on it and her unopened letter.

Then he put a match to the straw and watched the blaze.

Sammy's Well

Sammy Little had the smallholding we used to call Butty's Brook; but if there ever was a brook no sign of it remained during Sammy's occupation.

It was, in fact, a significant loss, for in a dry summer Sammy was hard put to find enough water for the needs of the holding. There was a so-called bottomless pond in one corner of the field that generally provided a contribution of murky black liquid but even this could be fallible.

One summer's morning in the early 'twenties Sammy's two huge sons, Efty and Bo, (perhaps Beau but this seems an unlikely nicety in that bucolic environment) took their pails to the pond as usual. Being slow both in movement and in comprehension they remained there for some time, absorbing the fact that the pond was sure enough empty.

"I'll be blowed," said Bo, personally aggrieved, "That ain't ever gone dry afore - not right dry."

"Hoo, that that ain't," agreed Efty. "I can't recollect that ever a-doin' that afore."

Old Sammy came hurrying across from the buildings, anxious because the stock had not been watered. Sammy was perennially anxious about some thing.

He took one look into the empty pond and swore.

"I don't recollect," repeated Efty for Sammy's benefit, "that ever happened afore."

"Well, that's happened now," said Sammy sourly, "And that 'ont git filled up agin by lookin' at it.

57

We'll atter git cartin' again. Put all the barrels in the cart and harness up."

When water shortage was desperate, Sammy and his boys would take a cartload of tubs to fill at a public pump or a nearby farm. As the days of drought continued such journeys became too frequent and time-wasting, beside straining relations with water-owning neighbours.

"We'll dig a well," Sammy told his two sons. "We'll be independent and hey our own water straight from a well. We'll hev it jest there." He drove a spade into the ground to make the spot only a few feet from the kitchen door.

"Where?" asked Efty eyeing the area from the temporary comfort of a seat on a spade handle.

"Jest here," repeated Sammy. He chopped into the ground again with the spade and Efty and Bo stared at the spot as if they expected a gush of water forthwith. A strong disinclination to become physically involved kept them unusually spry. "How big?" Bo asked.

"How dew I know - 'haps 50 feet afore we come to water."

"Ar, how big roundards, I mean."

Sammy judiciously pushed in two or three sticks around the mark he had made and Efty got off his spade handle and helpfully scored a rough circle with his boot. Then he got back.

"Tidy size," he said. "That need expert min for that job."

"Well, that's what I got," Sammy snarled. "I got yew an' I got Bo. Yew may not be experts yit but yew will afore yew finish."

"Ar," came from Bo. "But hev yew thought about that a-cavin' in. That ought to be shored up - or something."

"Shored up?" said Efty. "Yew atter shore up uppards. There ain't no way o' shorin' up downards."

"Well, that's a arse-ended sort o' job," opined Bo. "Tha's like doin' a job standin' on y'r hid. Anything sensible, that start at the bottom and finish at the top."

"Yeah," Efty agreed thoughtfully. "On'y that ain't feasible a-startin' at the bottom of a well - 'cept o' course ef yore a mole."

Such conversations between his two sons drove Sammy to a degree of exasperation bordering on violence and seeing the signs on their father's face, the two set to work with a semblance of willingness. There were soon problems, including that of disposing of the heap of soil taken from the hole. Sammy had an idea and ordered the two boys to clear out part of a boundary ditch with the intention of laying some drains in the bottom and dumping the unwanted soil on top. It was while Bo was scraping away at the bottom of the ditch that he unearthed the bones of what seemed to be a human skeleton.

"Why, that owd sod," Bo exclaimed to Efty. "He bin a lyin' there 'haps for centries an' no one knew he was there." The skull fascinated them. They stuck it gruesomely on a post, but having no devouring interest in anatomy generally, they shovelled the rest of the bones into a heap.

"He's bina lyin' there," Efty mused, " an' he ain't done a mite to help. Still, I reckon that ain't too late

59

to start."

Bo laughed. "He don't look in right good condition for heavy work."

"He'll work," Efty claimed. He and Bo loaded the bones on to the barrow while Sammy was feeding stock and tipped them all into the new well, which was still but a few feet deep.

"He 'ont go far till the mornin' then we'll git him out agin, very surprised and careful like. I reckon Sammy 'll dew the rest."

Sure enough, by noon next day, the two brothers were reaching for and dusting the bones carefully. placing them at the feet of an assorted group of onlookers including police, museum officials and general hangers on.

A little later, officialdom took over. The well was sealed, other excavations were started and complete restitution was promised in the form of a new, professionally-dug well. The skeleton itself was of little importance though mystifying for a time through having but one femur. It was eventually brought by Sammy's dog from the ditch, a fact which explained a great deal to Sammy and raised his estimation of his sons immensely.

The new well brought great improvement to the holding but little to Sammy's domestic habits. To the end of his life he held that the best flavoured cup of tea came from the pond in the corner of the field.

Maudie

M audie always came to the gate when she heard
anyone in the lane. People said that she was
forever listening for people to go past. When she came
out she stayed behind the old farm gate, half-hidden
by the tall post, but she watched carefully and smiled
to those she knew.

She was usually there when the children went to
school and sometimes stretched her hand through the
gate, holding an apple or a few cherries. Despite the
temptation, children seldom stayed to take the offering.

Parental suspicion of Maudie, for no more reason
than that she was single and lived alone, was unerring-
ly reflected in the children. It was part of the routine
of going to school to make an exaggerated dash past
the offending Maudie and her offerings, then turn and
shout rude remarks until they had turned the corner.

Maudie lived in the small brick farmhouse sur-
rounded by a jumble of timber buildings that was
dignified by the name of Mallet's Farm. It lay on the
narrow loop or back road between the two separate
parts of the village. There was almost a mile of this
wandering lane and only three houses on the entire
length.

The middle one was Mallet's Farm, where Maudie
lived, while the other two were occupied by a basket-
maker named Sam Storey and by a smallholder
turned pedlar whom everyone knew as Charlie. Since

the main street and shop stood at one end of the village while the church and school were at the other, most people made use of the back road and went by Charlie's and Maudie's and Sam's on the way.

Like Maudie, both of her neighbours lived alone, both in timber bungalows on a few acres of land. Charlie, the pedlar, had long ago sold some of his unwanted land to the basket-maker who needed it for growing osiers. Instead of working the soil, Charlie went out nearly every day with his horse and cart that carried every kind of kitchen requirement from pegs, candles and hearthstone to soap, vinegar and paraffin oil. Boys could buy marbles or tops or thick elastic for their catapults. Charlie's cart was welcome for miles around.

As for Sam, the basket-maker, he spent most of his time working in his shed or in the osier beds but once a week he piled his cart with new linen-baskets, bushel skeps and egg-baskets and took them to market.

As soon as Maudie heard the iron tyres of the carts on the road she would come out to watch them go and later, return. Charlie, who did not share the prejudices of the village people about Maudie, always waved cheerfully or stopped to bring candles and oil. But Sam made no more than the courteous acknowledgement of her presence. He carried back many of the white, new baskets from the market and seemed never to have sold enough to put him in good humour.

When he got to Maudie's gate his averted gaze was stern and melancholy. Maudie would watch him go past and then return to her lonely life in the house but on more than one occasion she had walked along the lane to Sam's holding and bought a basket for herself.

"I thought 'haps yew might ha' got one o' them little ow' barskets they put flarze in," she said. "Dew yew make 'em sort, Sam?"

Sam was flustered, what with unharnessing the horse and having a woman's company at the same time. "Cor-blast, I got every sort o' barsket yew c'n think on," he told her. "But I ain't got no flar barskets, whatever they may be."

Nevertheless Maudie found a basket that would be useful and took her time, despite his scornful silence, to examine the weaving shed and the other buildings before he disappeared into the house.

Although always treated as an outsider, even by Sam, Maudie was no stranger to the village. As a child she had been adopted by the Mallets who then farmed the holding. She was brought up by the hardworking pair and like them had spent her days labouring in the house and the fields. By the time that Mrs. Mallet died she was 30, roughened by hard work but still good looking. Only once had a young man had the temerity to visit her at the farm and then he had been chased off by old Mallet with a pitch fork. The gossips of the village did not omit to voice their suspicion that the old man had an eye on her himself.

When she was 40, old Mallet died and she was left alone. The farm was hers as well as a useful sum of money, but she made little attempt to cope, beyond caring for the animals. The hedges began to sprawl and cover themselves with old-man's-beard while the arable became all but lost to weeds. Even the fruit trees, the damsons and bullaces that stood along the roadside, were becoming hidden and the William pears allowed to grow so high only the wasps could now reach them. The neglect strengthened local opinion that Maudie was a simpleton - what with her odd little ways, her broad dialect and homely dresses. She seemed already to be an eccentric old maid.

In fact, Maudie's slight oddities were due only to her lack of commerce with the outside world. Her head, as others came to find, was "screwed on the right way."

One day in August, when the crab apples in the hedges were beginning to colour for the autumn, a man rode past Mallet's Farm on a bicycle. He rode past and came back, three or four times before he dismounted and pushed open the big gate. He had to knock three times at the farmhouse door before Maudie presented herself and demurely enquired his business.

"I don't 'spose yew remember me, Maudie?" he asked hopefully. "Tha's a long time agoo now, I'm Bob - Bob Small. The last time I come to see yew owd Mallet showed me the sharp ind o' his pitch-fork."

It was indeed the erstwhile admirer come to resume his courtship of 20 years before. Maudie registered her surprise and pleasure, as clever as a modern miss, since she had recognised him when he first passed and had found time to change her dress and assess the situation. She showed him over the farm, not omitting the signs of neglect, which, she agreed with Bob, needed a man about the place. Bob was delighted, both with Maudie's welcome and with the potential value of her property, and could hardly wait to begin a conventional courtship.

From then on, Maudie enjoyed a new respect in the village. Even the children showed deference to her, especially if her "young man" (Bob was 45) was in the vicinity. But Charlie, the pedlar, was quite put out. He had never thought of Maudie in this light before and he realised that he had missed an opportunity. He went across to confide in Sam, as he worked at his baskets in the weaving shed, his doubts about the motives and suitability of Bob Small as a husband for Maudie.

"That fare to me," Sam observed after some thought, "that ain't no concern o' ours, Maudie'll dew what she want to dew. That ain't our place to interfere. I reckon what yew should dew is try an' cut the other feller out."

"You're right," agreed Charlie. "I ought to ha' hung my hat up there long ago. Maudie c'n decide atwin the tew on us, then, Bob an' me." "Yeah, she'll decide," Sam said confidently. "She's owd enough an' - well, I was goin' to say ugly enough, but o' course she ain't that."

So it was that, during the autumn and winter of that year, Maudie was wooed alternately by the middle-aged Bob and by Charlie, while Sam prepared his osiers for the spring. Maudie sang in the house and no longer watched at the gate. By St. Valentine's Day, she decided, she would have to put her suitors out of their misery, but for the time being it was pleasant to enjoy the prestige and importance of so much admiration.

"St. Valentine's Day," she told them both, "I shall

make up my mind an' tell yew on St. Valentine's."

So she did. On the 14th February she walked down the lane to Sam's. The day was light and sharp with the promise of Spring. Sam stopped weaving and looked at her.

"Are yew a'coming?" she asked gently. "Yew ha' waited long enough."

Jack Watson

No one could have said for certain that Jack Watson had come home to die. It was something that one felt afterwards, when you put together all the circumstances. Not that many people were concerned, one way or another, since only a handful of villagers knew him. But old Ezra remembered him; he knew all the facts. Ezra was the old man who, when Jack Watson was a boy, always used to be at the smithy. He sat in the forge by the fire, generally. He did not work there but came from the thin comfort of his cottage to sit where there was warmth and activity.

There was a stool or something in the corner just out of reach of the smith's elbow when he was pumping the bellows and Ezra would sit there contentedly for hours at a time.

There was always something going on — the shaping of horse-shoes on the anvil or making a new link for a chain; sometimes the fixing of a new iron tyre on to a wagon wheel in the yard. Ezra watched it all, smoking an old pipe almost burned down through lighting it with hot irons from the fire.

To Jack Watson, who was a mere boy then and came often to peep in at the forge on his way home from school, Ezra must have seemed an old, old man, though in fact he could not have been more than sixty at that time.

One day, when the forge seemed full of sparks and

noise, Ezra pulled the boy out of the way and into the corner beside him.

"Dew yew stand heah, o' partner, out o' the way," Ezra told him. "That don't hut, yew watchin' — s'long as yew keep out o' their way." And on many occasions after, Jack shared the privileged corner with old Ezra, while the smith got on with his work and made no comment at all.

So it happened that Ezra was the last of the local people to see Jack before he had run away from home when he was 14 — and 15 years later he was practically the only person to recognise and speak to him on the day that he returned.

It was a day in early June when Jack came back to his native village, half puzzled himself as to why he should do so. During the past few months so many other things had required his attention. First, the worries of his failing business, then the shock of the rift that had ensued between him and his wife and the eventual separation.

Now, after weeks of pain and worry he seemed to have reached a plateau of numbness, where his only thoughts were irrelevant and nebulous.

He could no longer think of his work or of his wife, twin subjects that had occupied the whole of his existence; instead he remembered how the forge bellows had roared when he was a boy and how the dog roses looked on the hedges under the Suffolk sky. Some compulsion required him to travel back to the certainties of his boyhood.

The village, he found when he arrived, was just as he remembered it, and yet different in that he seemed to be no part of it. For all its familiarity, it rejected him. Almost he felt like leaving again, straight away, to forget it completely. But then he remembered the river. At least he could look at the river before he went and remember the summer Sunday afternoons long ago when it seemed the whole village population walked the river path.

That was a different world, if you like! When you were dressed and polished for Sunday it had been an occasion to walk beside the river and encounter friends and acquaintances, whole families or solitary beauties. Like Connie.

Connie — and there was Alice too. He had loved them both on alternate weeks but forgotten them both long ago. He walked back from the river and through the main street. Once, he remembered, when you used to walk, the old houses would seem to lean down and listen to your footsteps — now they shrank back from the noise of the traffic.

Once or twice as he walked he thought he saw a face that he knew and a name would jerk up in his memory, but no one recognised him. He had no place here nor even an identity. He had a kind of panic suddenly as if he were a lost child, then stirred himself to seek out other places that were familiar.

There was the sweet shop, the school, the pump — all there, but they gave him nothing back for his prolonged stare, their comfort was no longer for him. But there was still the forge. Of course, the forge and old Ezra! He would help him to come back.

When he turned the corner towards the forge, the panic returned. He could not recognise it — all the changes there had been; the new buildings, the traffic signs. He leaned against the wall, steadying himself against the confusion, telling himself that he would find the forge soon enough. Anyway, old Ezra had lived in this row of houses — perhaps he would seek him out first.

Ezra was indeed at home, though bound to his chair by age and its frailties, and Jack Watson was grateful for even this tenuous contact.

"Yes. I remember yew," the old man said steadily. "Yew allust used ter come in the smithy. They say yew ran off, left yar hoom an' yar foolks, ter git on in the world. But 'ere, tha's all over an' done wi' now. I reckon yew're on a sort o' holiday 'en?"

Jack Watson shook his head; he was anxious that the old man should understand. "I've come back — back, to start agin. I always did have it in my mind that I would come back. All the time I was away I thought that if everything else failed I could come back and start again. But I can't. That's funny, I can see all the places I knew, an' the people — but I can't touch 'em. They're out o' reach somehow."

The old man considered. "That take time," he granted. "Yew hatter grow yar roots agin. Tha's like this - yew grow a seed in yar garden an' that'll grow an' fit in wi' all the other plants. But dew yew once pull that plant out tha's a rum job a-gittin' it ter settle in agin."

"The point is — I never really wanted to go away," Jack Watson remembered. "That was my father — we was always quarrelling. I had to go, sooner or later."

"Ah, but yew see, yew did go," old Ezra pointed out. "Yew saw things, learned things, — that ain't easy to go back to nothen. See, I don't hanker arter things cos I don't know any better. But my wife —

70

yew know when she was alive she was allust hankerin'."

"She used ter work as a house-parlourmaid an' that was the biggest trial o' har life cos we cou'n't afford no bone china. Anytime anyone come to the house she'd say 'I hoope yew don't mind if I don't git out my bone china."

"She fretted over that. I din't cos I din't know no better."

"Well, we'll see. Anyway, I'll call in at the old forge while I'm here."

"Yew'll have a job t'dew that," Ezra objected, "Cos that's bin took down this five year."

It seemed odd to Ezra when he looked back that Jack Watson never seemed to grasp that the forge was gone. During the few days that he stayed in the village and throughout the several conversations that they had together, he seemed unwilling or unable to comprehend.

Perhaps it was because it was the last of the tangible things he remembered to which he could cling.

In the end, perhaps, Jack Watson did indeed find the forge. Two days after his last conversation with Ezra he was found dead seated in the old lych-gate outside the church.

Knowing how he had searched, Ezra came to believe that he had discovered something — a recognition, a return to grace.

Indeed, there were Jack Watson's initials cut into the oak beside him that he had done when he was a boy.

Whether it was this, or whether he had thought he

71

had at last found the forge, it was impossible to know, but something had finally brought him home.

Jacob and the Medsun

"Tha's like this hare, master," said Jacob carefully, as if anxious to be scrupulously fair about his condition. "I don't fare tew bad nor I ain't altogither roight, ef yew know what I mean. I'm jist sort o' fair to middlin' moost days. I reckon tha's what come o' bein' born tew sune."

Needless to say, he was on his way to the dispensary. He seemed generally to be on the way to the dispensary or going away from it, or off to the chemist for a mixture, or sitting and taking a little needed sustenance in the corner of the bar at the Cow and Bells.

His middling health was a matter of considerable study for Jacob in the years of his retirement. There was no doubt that though no malingerer, he enjoyed his visits to the dispensary and the frequent inquiries as to his well-being.

In the course of time he had become something of an oracle on medicines to more transient patients and would take it on himself to advise any who sat beside him in the cold comfort of the dispensary waiting room.

"Dew yew ask for some o' that green medsun," he would say, tapping his nearest neighbour on the knee. "Tha's good stuff, master. Don't yew take 'at 'ere pink. He allst give me green if I ask'm. Let him go ahid a-telling yew the yarn then when he go to start mixin' the stuff yew say howd yew hard owd

73

pardner. I'd ruther hev the green."

Then he would go on to tell of his experience at the hospital a few years before.

"Them doctors - they ha' got ut up here, master. There ain't nothen they miss. Tha's wonderful what they know nowadays. They got to wark on me when I went up to that horsepital an' they turned everythin' inside out a-lookin' for ut. They cou'n't find ut what they was a-lookin' for but they tunned everythin' inside out then put ut back agin."

"I reckon that done me a master lot o' good. I bin middlin' ever since, but for me rheumatics. That start hollerin' somtimes — I don't take no notice o' that, tha's jist the owd boons a-gittin' set."

Jacob became so proprietorial about his green medicine that when he came across an itinerant quack doctor one day in the Cow and Bells, he felt bound to criticise.

The quack had had the effrontery, it seemed to Jacob, not only to occupy his corner at the bar but actually to display several bottles of dark-looking liquid on the counter. Gummed labels, smudged with ink, sought to prove how efficacious the mixture would be for anyone with a pain or indeed any physical problem.

Jacob snorted sceptically at the bottles and since he had at that moment returned from the dispensary, took his bottle of green medicine from his pocket and stood it pointedly beside the alien brew.

Perhaps, as it turned out, he would have done better to take a more modest stand on such an arguable matter but having thrown down the gauntlet he had to prepare for battle.

The quack doctor, a stranger who came to the neighbourhood once or twice a year at the time of the fair, was a large, seedy and ruthless looking individual who immediately took umbrage at the sight of the green medicine.

"You drink this?" he asked in affected surprise. "You like peppermint-flavoured water?"

Jacob indignantly snatched at the bottle to recover it but the big man was holding it high above his head and then making a show of shaking it and sniffing the contents.

"You must either be quite incurable, old man, that they give you sugar-water or there is nothing wrong with you. It is just a placebo."

"Yew can call that what names yew loike, master," said Jacob, enraged as much by the man's "posh" voice as by his foreign vocabulary, "that dew me good. Tha's wunnerful strong stuff. Tha's more'n I could say for them bottles yew got."

"It's a placebo," the man repeated. "To keep you amused, like a dummy. If you have any pain, it would do you no good."

"What about this hare rubbage, 'en," snorted Jacob, stung into an unusual nastiness. He picked up one of his rival's bottles. "I guarantee there ain't nothen in hare I can't beat."

The man was on the point of replying in like manner when he stopped and his manner changed.

"I admire you, sir," he told Jacob, "for standing up for something you believe in. You'd recommend that fine green mixture to anybody, eh?"

Jacob felt that it would be unfriendly to refuse the drinks that the stranger called for, and for the next hour he was led through a maze of sales-talk that only became more confusing as time went on.

It seemed that the quack actually wanted him to recommend his medicine and in his surprise he readily agreed to distribute bottles exactly like his own which the man would provide.

"I think you have a wonderful mixture there," the quack conceded. "And, if I may say so, you have a wonderful way of recommending it. I am in a position to help you. I want you to sell the green mixture to all your friends. It will cost them half-a-crown. But I could make it for you at eighteen-pence a bottle. Tha's a shilling a bottle profit and the satisfaction of helping your friends. You shall have a hundred bottles by Wednesday."

It must be said that, from the start, Jacob did not really like the idea but could find nothing wrong with the logic of the transaction or with the profits.

It was with growing doubts that Jacob returned to the Cow and Bells on Wednesday and carried away on his wheelbarrow two large baskets packed with straw in which the efficacious potion lay, and paid over the cash.

He was now, as the quack reminded him, a businessman in his own right, with a product he believed in and the right to sell to whoever would buy.

From the very first the bottles were an embarrassment.

To his surprise, his friends were able to restrain any unseemly haste in the matter of buying the mixture and he went on his way more than a little conscious of the glances that were passed.

In his cottage, Jacob set out all the bottles on the dresser and was staggered by the sheer size of his business undertaking. He took three or four bottles immediately to his neighbours who had always shown an admiration for his green medicine. They were duly impressed but were unable to buy a bottle just then.

"Yew take 'at 'ere bottle, that'll dew yew good," said Jacob, who felt that it accorded with the high tradition of medicine to provide the cure and seek reward later.

At the end of the day he had sold three bottles at cost price and given two away. He had also, unfortunately, exhausted his list of acquaintances.

Jacob spent the next day eyeing the remaining 95 bottles and found that they had changed from something good and beneficial to objects that proclaimed his cupidity and weakness. He was ashamed of quack salemanship, of his own hypochondria, of his stupidity generally, and of green medicine in particular. There was only one way of regaining his self-respect. He packed the medicine bottles back into the baskets and waited for the fair.

Three months had to go by before the Green was visited again by the roundabouts and sideshows but then, sure enough, the quack doctor was present with his stall. On the day that the fair opened and when the locals were beginning to gather, Jacob set up a complete display of his bottles close beside the quack doctor's stall. Beneath it was a poster done by Jacob himself.

FREE (it said). THIS RUBBAGE WAS MADE BY THIS QUACK HERE AN THAT AIN'T NO USE TO ANYBODY.

In no time wrong was righted and Jacob set off home with his barrow, as relieved to get rid of the bottles as for the return of his stake money.

When he remembered he had put his own genuine mixture in with the other, he was glad of that, too. It would be some time before he needed the dispensary again.

Easter Fair

"Tha's a fat lot o' use," said Sid, meaning there was no use at all. "Tha's a fat lot o' use yew a-carryin' on like 'at. Yew 'a' alust bin a-tellin' me to go - well now I a' gone. I arn't a' coming back no more.

Sid had chosen the garden gate for making his parting remarks. In the cottage doorway stood his in-laws, Joe and Mary Sawyer, and behind them the sobbing figure of their daughter Vera, who was Sid's wife.

The conclusion that Sid was being driven out was in fact true, but under such provocation and by such kindly people that the listening neighbours who long remembered the incident, knew full well that Sid himself was to blame.

Since he had married Vera, two years ago, he had fastened himself like a parasite upon the family, draining their resources and their patience.

Joe Sawyer had long ago given up trying to persuade Sid to get a job and the situation became so unendurable that eventually he was told that he must go - to get a job and a home and then to send for Vera to join him.

During these uncomfortable developments Vera herself could do little more than weep, torn between two sides. Now, suddenly, on an Easter Monday evening, Sid had apparently decided to take his noisy departure.

Mary was upset too. "Tha's sech a funny way to go,"

79

she said worriedly, while her husband Joe kept a grim silence "jest a-goin' off like that."

"How d'yew want me to go, ma?" shouted Sid rudely. "There's a ruddy grut drum in the attic - why don't yew git that a-goin'?" Now he hesitated. "Well, yew allust towd me to clear out - so tha's what I'm a-goin' to do. Don't yew try an' stop me 'cos that ain't no use."

"I 'ont stand in your way, bor," Joe said hastily, seeing Sid's resolution waning. "Ef tha's how yew feel, du yew git away afore tha's dark."

Seeing no help for it now but to put on a good face, Sid tore himself away and slammed the gate behind him. For once true to his word, he never returned to the cottage again and later it was learned that he had joined up with the travelling fair that always set up on the common at Easter time.

At that time, about the end of the 1914-18 War, an acute shortage of housing had caused the government to provide a grant for private building. This allowed country people who wished to use their own initiative to build a house of their own - often of timber, with a weather-board exterior and a roof of corrugated iron or asbestos.

One of the necessities of such a project however, was a brick-built chimney and this was held to be the work of a specialist. One such expert was Joe Sawyer. He was a man of uncertain age, with a flowing beard and a prophet-like aspect who, despite his rather slow progress in a donkey-pulled dog-cart, gave the impression of great and urgent haste. He would puff and fuss, blowing his whiskers this way and that, and would jump into his little cart and disappear again at the slightest provocation.

Such a manner persuaded many people that he was the expert he pretended to be; in fact, his chimneys were more often than not disastrous mistakes. Smoking fireplaces were a regular legacy of his ministrations, and more than one of the timber bungalows had to have the kitchen window open whenever there was a fire, which in those days was almost permanently.

After the job was finished Joe became even more hurried and elusive, and if he were cornered he would give the matter of excessive smoke his gravest consideration and advise a cowl on the chimney. Or, if this had already been tried, he would advise burning out the chimney with an armful of straw, a process which sometimes all but set the timber bungalow alight.

Besides his Biblical appearance there was another factor that kept Joe in business. This was his wife, Mary, whose hospitality and charm caused many a village neighbour to call at the cottage on a Sunday evening on the pretext of seeing Joe but really to be asked to sit down to one of Mary's famous suppers.

Cold meat and pickles, home-made bread and beer were on the table - but the enjoyment came chiefly from the presence of the hostess, in herself a kind of benediction for the meal. She showed that food was something to be happy over as well as to be thankful for.

On such occasions Joe would say little; conversation was almost entirely with Mary. In a way she was a public relations cover for Joe and his failures and I came to believe that she knew how imcompetent he really was and was protecting him. Sometimes Vera appeared at the table, pale and quiet, but visitors knew better than to say a word about her unhappy marriage.

In the year that followed Sid's departure, Joe and Mary did their best to ease their daughter's unhappiness though with little success until she received a short and grubby letter from Sid, followed by two others.

At this she began to cheer up and as the year went by became almost her old self again.

When Easter came, and the travelling fair returned to the village, she was off to the common in a hurry as soon as the organ began.

In an hour she was back at the cottage, unhappy but determined, packed a case and was gone, running blindly out of the door to avoid the agony of the farewells.

The Sawyers watched her go and waited, listening to the blare of the fairground music until it, too, stopped and the fair departed.

Soon people came to supper again and Joe built more smokey chimneys and the years passed.

Only at Easter time was there a change in the routine. The cottage would be shut and the curtains drawn . . . and no one knew what Joe and Mary did or thought as the music of the organ came over the common from the travelling fair.

Grandfather's Wedding

At his wedding my grandfather put a miniature whip in the lapel of his coat for fun. It was the sign of his calling and he had worn it at the hiring fair when, years before, he had crossed the Waveney and settled for good among the southern folk.

The hiring was to Mr. Mayhew, of Valley Farm, for one year, but grandfather never had to be hired again.

He had found what he sought - a good farm and a fair boss - and more besides, for it was at Valley Farm that he met and fell in love with Annie.

She was house-parlourmaid in the farmhouse and in a position superior to the other servants. That was why grandfather was surprised to find her one day in the dairy bare to the elbows and scouring out the separator. For once his concern overcame his shyness.

"Yew han't ought to dew that, miss," he said. "Tha's dutty owd wark."

She looked at him with a flash of the spirit he came to love and mimicked his dialect.

"Well, I've got dutty owd hands." She held them up, smiling. "They'll wash. In fact, I'm helping Emily so we can both get off duty together."

Very soon it was Grandfather and not Emily that she arranged to meet.

During the harvest that preceded the wedding - the true precedence of country life - Annie would slip away from the house and down to the fields in her modest black dress that was the afternoon uniform.

83

She would watch as he worked or make bands of straw for the tying up of sheaves and when all the corn carting was done she bent regularly for the gleaning. Within the same orbit of farmhouse and buildings the two worked together, sometimes within sight and sound of each other, always with a satisfaction from the other's presence that lightened the dull burden of their labour.

When the harvest was over and the tumbrils began to cart out the manure from the yards they went together to church and were married.

It was a ceremony that sealed both their union and their status in the village community as indicated by the Rector in reminding them to thank God for keeping them in that state of life to which they had been born.

Grandfather said afterwards that he wouldn't have minded keeping his part of the bargain if God had kept his - for in the bleak years to come they were all but driven by poverty into the nearby workhouse.

But all this was in the future. Today was their wedding day and when the service was over the bride and bridegroom led the way from the church down the lane to their cottage while friends and neighbours and sundry children followed in a straggling, but hilarious procession.

At the head of the procession would be grandfather, strong and confident as a favoured worker at Valley Farm.

And others, with watch chains looped across waistcoats of good lasting cloth, shouting to their wedding-prim wives to avoid the cowpat and to look at young Harry with his arm already around Amy's silk sashed waist.

Behind came the children, stumbling and giggling in excitement in their long clothes, sending their flowered bonnets awry and pink ribbons flying before ever they reached the end of the lane.

In the cottage more people would be waiting and the food and beer set ready on the table in the parlour, that was used only for occasions such as this.

No need to lift the latch today - the wicket gate stands open and the front door too, and the September sun not so warm that it kept the visitors from crowding noisily into the tiny rooms.

Yet something in the nature of the occasion kept the sexes separate, the women huddling together over details and gossip and the men soon becoming uncomfortable in the confines of the house and moving out into the open to play pitch and toss along the garden path.

Soon, an argument arose over weight-lifting, a prime topic in days of manual farmwork, and Grandfather and Bill Gant looked around for objects to try their strength on.

The chopping block was a mere bagatelle; the shoe-mending last something that they could toss up in the air.

"Tell yew what," said Grandfather, finishing his third mug of beer, "there's owd Bessie there in the sty, an' she's about 16 stoon. Ef yew can lift her I'll give yew best."

The hefty pig, reared by Grandfather in preparation for married life, was cornered but proved to be poor lifting material. At the third try it rushed out of the sty, knocked Bill Gant into the hedge and was through a gap and into the churchyard in a moment.

"She 'ont go far," said Grandfather following it through the gap, "cos there ain't no way out o' the chu'chyard." In the churchyard the two men were reminded of their original quest. In a corner were two discarded tombstones, no longer in use as monuments but thrown together for paving.

"Them tew stoons," said Bill, "they're about the same size. I bet I can carry one further 'n yew can carry the other."

With difficulty the heavy stones were lifted, placed on head and shoulders and they began to walk unsteadily along the gravel path until confronted by the Rector.

Grandfather tried to touch his forelock as usual, but the gravestone wobbled and he quickly grabbed hold of it again.

The Rector had much to say and it seemed disrespectful to remove their heavy loads until he had finished.

They were almost on their knees when he concluded, "And what I came to tell you was that your pig is in the Rectory garden eating my cabbages. I would remind you that this is Glebe land" - he sounded the 'Glebe' as if it were the clarion call of Gabriel himself - "and you are on Glebe land, you live in a Glebe house and I am a Glebe commissioner."

"Yes Sir," said Grandfather. "Yes, Mr. Glebe," said Bill stupidly.

Grandfather all but lost his job and his cottage over his wedding-day misconduct but gradually the affair was forgotten.

When the Rector came to visit the cottage in a mood of conciliation, Grandfather had the impression that

whereas God and the Rector were not all that put out,
it would take a lot of church-going to placate the Glebe.

The Hero

I n the winter of 1944 a War Ag. lorry used to hurry along the quiet roads early in the morning carrying the local labour gang from their warm beds to the cold comfort of the sugar beet fields.

Under the green canvas hood sat twelve men wrapped in a variety of coats and sacking aprons. They were of the less-important of wartime's manpower, being mostly old men and those discharged from the Forces.

The most distinguishable character, by his great bulk and growling voice, was an ex-regular seaman known as Tiny, who always claimed the best seat near the tailboard.

They all sat silent on these journeys, as if they had long ago said all they wanted to say - all of them, that is, except the new man recently discharged from the Army.

When the lorry arrived at the field the foreman-driver would immediately measure the width of the rows and pace out their length, study the size and population of the beet and make calculations on a piece of paper. The men would drop their lunch bags along the hedgerow and begin to sharpen their narrow-bladed toppers.

"That look like takin' work today," muttered one as he watched the foreman. They all waited resentfully, suspicious of the foreman's calculations and his superior powers. A gipsy-looking man with a rasping voice brought out some spicey adjectives for taking-work, not so much from disagreement than as a general comment on all work.

"We'll take 'em," said the foreman, coming up. "If we keep at it and the weather hold we could make ten bob extra on the day."

"Takin'-work!" The men spat and grumbled in protest but took up their separate positions between two rows of beet. Piecework they always objected to on principle though it made little difference in effect since they always worked at the same pace. It was something that stirred a kind of peasant obstinacy and even when they received their larger pay-packets, it made no difference to their attitude.

In the cold morning light the men bent and began to pull the beet, one in each hand, and banging them together in the same movement, threw them in a row. They would not look up again until they reached the opposite hedge. It was what they had done yesterday and would do again tomorrow, every day of fair weather or foul from the beginning of October to the end of December.

Only the new man had anything to say. He was a chirpy little character named Keeter, a veritable sparrow as he worked beside the massive Tiny. He was full of war exploits, escapes and captures, in most of which he seemed to have been the leading figure. Tiny listened in silence but at bait time when sitting under the hedge he growled to the others: "I'll hull that little owd pipny into the pond ef he don't shut up."

As the morning wore on the temperature rose a little. Hands that had been red and raw from plunging into the wet leaves became dry and the men less disgruntled.

In the half hour dinner break they sat in the lorry. Tiny found Keeter beside him again and listened to his tales with obvious scorn.

"You ought to be a ruddy field-marshal, mate, not a corporal," he commented. Some of the men laughed. Even among the mixed humanity that formed the labour gang, the new man looked meagre and contemptible. He was thin, scraggy and almost bald. His old khaki tunic and trousers seemed far too big for his shrunken body. As he talked his eyes shifted restlessly and his hands were forever picking and prying.

In the afternoon the weather held good and it looked as if the piecework would yield a handsome bonus. The little man Keeter worked with a nervous energy beside Tiny and continued to tell him stories. He was the last man from Dunkirk, he said, and the first in Narvik. He had seen Monty twice in North Africa. He had been honoured for his gallantry and given the George Medal by the King.

When they reached the hedge Tiny said to the foreman: "For God's sake take that little runt out of my way, or I'll kill him."

"Why don't you shut up?" The foreman turned on the little man. "You're on'y a little cog in a bloddy grut war like everybody else."

The rest of the men had reached the hedge and were preparing to work back again, this time hooking and topping the beet they had pulled. Tiny was growling: "He's a born liar. He's bin to places no other Englishman's bin tew. He's even bin talkin' to the King."

Suddenly the little man threw down his chopper and

pulled himself up straight. In dramatic absurdity, he solemnly saluted. "So I did," he shouted like a hero in a film, "I spoke to His Majesty the King an' he said he was pleased to reward me for my gallantry in action."

"You silly clot," said Tiny in disgust, making a stumbling lunge towards him. "What the hell are you saluting for?"

"Because I'm a patriot," said the little man, "and proud of it."

Tiny made another move towards him and Keeter backed into the hedge, slipped and fell through a gap into the ditch. He lay still for a minute and the foreman came up and gave him a hand to get out. He was wet through and had to go into the lorry to dry off with an old sack. He was quiet for the rest of the day and he never came again.

The gang finished the field and moved on to another farm. A few weeks later they learned that the little man had died because of war wounds he had received. No one in the gang felt it his duty to go to the funeral but they heard afterwards that it had been an exceptional affair with some high-ranking officers in the cortège and a George Medal on the coffin.

Stanley and the Kids

The day of the Treat was the best in all the summer. Even if it rained there would be a marquee for shelter and the big house itself would offer its cloistered verandahs for village people to stand in - but it hardly ever did.

Nearly always the Treat came on a day that blazed with June sunshine, when the whole park was a sea of golden buttercups and white bull-daisies. It was a day when the lark sang over the countryside and into our simple living.

The Treat could not have been held at a happier spot - which was not at the village rectory but at the stately manor house three miles away - because here there was peace and excitement and grandeur.

Here you could glimpse the fringe of the elegant life of the gentry, so delicate that the immense kitchen gardens were tucked away in walled areas at the back so that the baser functions of the earth in providing the food should be out of sight.

In the front of the manor were the pleasure gardens with the terraces and rustic urns, with rose gardens and sweeping lawns that led to the shrubberies and the lake.

On a fine day in June it was a wonderful place. You could sit on the lawn and eat strawberries and cream while the children ran races and scrambled madly for sweets. You could sample the aristocratic command of views over the fields with your friends and neighbours, for everyone was welcome and all who cared to go were carried there on farm waggons belonging to the manor farms.

Nearly everyone did go. At two o' clock in the afternoon the waggons and horses decorated with fluttering ribbons and new rosettes would stand alongside the green ready for the journey.

Old people would be helped aboard and given seats while the children clambered up over the wheels and sat on the clean straw on the floor. Everyone was conscious of wearing best clothes, of Sunday sashes and straw hats, new sailor suits and stiff Norfolk jackets. In an ecstasy of anticipation they would set off along the quiet roads.

Perhaps there were only two people that day who were not entirely blissful at the prospect of the Treat. One was the colonel himself, who occupied himself during the morning roping off some of the more vulnerable of the manorial flower-beds.

The other was Stanley, the 13 year-old member of the overflowing Gates family, who was morose for private reasons - he was in love.

He knew he was in love though it was something he did not want to mention, least of all to the object of his devotion. It was just a feeling he had in his stomach every time he saw her.

He had not even dared to follow her into the same waggon but he knew without looking how she sat and how she laughed and how she took off her hat to show her long golden hair. He could feel how she looked and the feeling was deep in his stomach.

"Little ow' Stan - he fare properly quiet today," commented one of the grown ups sitting way up on the hard seats. "Well, 'haps he ha' fell in love," squealed someone else. But his mother said: "Tha's his injigestion, I reckon - the way he dew eat. He's tew quiet to take notice o' them young mawthers."

"Quiet waters run deep," squawked some old woman, but Stanley took little notice of the remarks until some boy called out, "Lizzie Gant, Lizzie Gant," Stanley flung himself upon the boy in a fury and they were still scuffling in the straw when the waggons reached the manor park.

Now there were other excitements to engage them. What with the stalls and the gardens, the incredibly vast, green lawns, the Celestion Brass Band pumping out its welcoming overture all over the sun-lit grounds, the noise and activity became intense.

Only Stanley took himself off from the rest and wandered down by the lake. There he took off his boots and stockings and dipped his feet into the cool, clear water, trying to pierce the bright reflection to discover if there were any fish.

A gang of children came racing down to the lake, Lizzie Gant among them. They swarmed on to the planks that stretched over the water and Lizzie went to the very edge and knelt down to look and her hair made a clear, yellow moon in the water.

"Pull me up," she shouted, and he was the first to grab her hand. She knows, he thought. But he could not bring himself to chase after her with the others.

Then, as he pulled on his boots there was another sound behind him. It was the colonel, dutifully jolly but watchful as usual.

"H'lo Stanley," he said. "Caught any big fish yet?"

Stanley scrambled to his feet, touched his forehead

in respect and mumbled something, in a daze as to how the colonel even knew his name.

"I've just had a word with your mother," said the colonel. He was looking at Stanley critically, weighing him up. Stanley stood up straight and pulled off his hat. "You're leaving school I hear, and want a job. Well as it happens I've got the very job for you. How would you like to be backhouse boy here at the manor, eh? Live in as well?"

"Yes sir, I would sir," Stanley managed to say.

"Right and the sooner the better eh? Well, come with me and I'll hand you over to Mr. Parks. He'll show you round. Start work on Monday."

Stanley followed the tall figure across the lawns. People stared, including Lizzie, but Stanley cared nothing for that. He was about to enter the colonel's service.

At the back of the manor the colonel entered what seemed to be a labyrinth of passages and called out: "Parks!" and the butler appeared from somewhere like a jack-in-the-box.

"This is Stanley," the colonel said brusquely. "Show him around."

Parks wrung his dry hands until the colonel had gone, then, as if he had got hold of something distasteful that he wanted to get rid of, he led Stanley disdainfully to the scullery. There was a girl in the scullery, a little older than Stanley, scrubbing down the great white table in the centre.

"I'll show yer," said Rosie. She had a little cap on her head and a neat uniform. Though only 14 she had been in the scullery long enough to acquire a cheerful authority that made Stanley fall in love all over again.

"The fust thing every mornin' yew atter clean all the boots an' shoes. Then the knives."

She showed him how to work the patent knife cleaner though Stanley was watching her soft, bare arms rather than the machine. "Then yew clean out the boilers and sift the ashes."

She paused and looked at him. "On'y we atter dew all our work in here. We don't go in the kitchen. Mr. Parks or the parlourmaid bring the shoes down to the kitchen an' Elsie the kitchen maid bring 'em in here."

"Same with the coal scuttles. When yew fill the scuttles yew stand 'em along the wall here. Elsie come an' take 'em into the kitchen, then Mr. Parks or the footman take 'em through."

After he left the scullery, the front lawns seemed a mass of excited activity. He found his mother sitting with her friends close by the band.

"I got the job," he said. "I'm going to be backus boy at the manor."

His mother was pleased. Her friends nodded sagely. "Yew can't beat service in a big house," they said.

Stanley watched the activity and listened to the music. He was not worried by the strange domestic hierarchy of the rich and only wanted to please Rosie.

"Omaha, Omaha," he sang out loud in tune with the band.

Lizzie and her gang came racing up. She was looking at Stanley and one of the boys pushed her against him. But Stanley took no notice.

His mother found a place for him among the grown-ups, and he sat there in new-found contentment and dignity.

When the boys pushed Lizzie towards him again he looked down at them with contempt.

"They're on'y kids," he told his mother.

The Swap

V era bustled out of the car with her shopping bag as soon as Frank pulled up in the main square of their local town. "Don't yew git out, Dad", she told him. "No point in both of us a-traipsin' around - an' I'll be quicker on my own."

Thankfully Frank sat for a few minutes in the car until the old stiffness in his legs drove him out to walk on the pavement for a bit. It was market day and the square was awash with traffic - the smell and the fuss of modern life in miniature, he thought resentfully. When you were old the noise and excitement of modern life seemed only purposeless; more, it was destructive, of quiet and of reality itself. He had known the little town and the square all his life and its character had gone and it was choked.

It wasn't only the traffic, he fretted. The buildings had all been tarted up and made to look better than they really were - just like the people, all trying to keep up with somebody else.

Across there, right opposite if only you could see it properly for parked cars, was where old Tom Payne lived long ago in the early twenties. The town was poor then and Tom's house, like many another, needed a coat of paint perhaps, but it was real and there was no pretence.

Old Tom Payne himself had been the finest tailor for miles. You could see him through the window sitting on the bare boards of the parlour that was his shop and gentry would come and seek him out for the privilege of wearing the clothes he made. He worked in a cold, disdainful fever until the job was done and paid for and then he drank continuously until the money was gone.

Now the same room where Tom had worked had become a frothy pink art shop. Once at least, thought Frank, a real artist had been there; poor, drunken, gifted Tom Payne. The thought that the old and simpler standards were dying depressed him. He wished he had not come into town today.

✻ ✻ ✻

The square was deserted. It was noon on a day in July, 1924, and nothing stirred. The old houses leaned and dozed in the sun and the church awoke only long enough to tell the hour. From Tom Payne's house young Georgie emerged and found that the steps were warm and inviting. He sat down carefully, each hand occupied with a hunk of bread that was mountainous with blackberry jam.

He rocked as he ate, watching the station drayhorse where it had been left tethered beside the water-trough similarly occupied with the contents of its nosebag.

Two men cycled placidly by on their way home to their midday meal. Georgie's friend appeared from somewhere on his bike and executed some hair-raising acrobatics all over the open space before whisking himself away again out of sight.

Georgie shouted to him, then finished his bread and jam and dozed, his eyes still on the horse. Across the other side of the square a man was standing. Georgie was surprised when he caught sight of him

99

for he had not noticed him arrive.

It was rather odd seeing someone just standing there and not anyone he knew and not going to or from work. He twisted over on the steps to pull the bag of marbles out of his corduroy trousers' pocket.

"Dad ain't in," he shouted across, remembering that this was one of his father's non-working days. "Dad ain't in," he repeated with less certainty as the man looked and said nothing.

Georgie's friend came racing back into the square and swirled and swiggled till Georgie held up his bag of marbles and then he suddenly braked and dropped his bike where it stood.

The two boys examined their marble collections to find their best shooting alleys and began to play a local version of the game. There came a time when a reckless throw took Georgie's prize alley almost across the square. The man was still standing there, an oldish man with grey hair.

"Dad ain't in," Georgie said again, then since the man made no answer, added rudely, "Why don't yew go on hoom, yew don't b'long here".

The man had taken a brightly coloured toy from his pocket and was holding it out to them. It was the sort of cheap plastic model of a space machine that was to become familiar in the breakfast cereal decades to come. The boys had seen nothing like it. They came nearer, fascinated by the unexplainable shape and meaning of it.

"Give y' my alley for that?" suggested Georgie. The man held out the toy and Georgie grabbed it from his hand, running off with his friend, until their curiosity overcame them in the middle of the square and they bent their heads together to touch and comprehend the thing. There was something in the shape and feel of it that awed and frightened them.

Suddenly Georgie threw the toy down in a panic of revulsion, stamping on it, trying to stamp out its vile insidious perfection. "Kill it", he said. He and his friend kept jumping on the toy in a kind of destructive delight until the plastic yielded and they kicked the pieces into the gutter.

"I know," shouted Georgie, hating and resenting the man who still stood there, "I know - he's a cheapjack!"

His friend whooped in agreement. "A cheapjack! You're on'y an owd cheapjack. Clear off an' take your rubbish," they chanted.

"It weren't worth the swap," said Georgie. His friend had doubts. "You can't go back on a swap," he said. "You'll atter give him the alley".

Georgie considered, then bent down and bowled the alley carefully along the ground. It came over the dry dust and clinked against the cobble stones before it came to rest at the feet of the man standing on the pavement and he stooped to pick it up.

✡ ✡ ✡

Vera was there asking if he was all right and noise came back in a great wave and the square receded again under the traffic. She ushered him back to the car, busy and anxious for his welfare. "You were dreaming again" she said, "stepping into the road like that. You ought to have kept in the car."

Frank sat back quietly in his seat as Vera took the car carefully through the maze and past the lights and the signs into the open country. "So are we all," he was thinking to himself - "all of us cheapjacks in these days. But it was all I had, all I had".

Potter's Green

One thing that you could not possibly miss in our village was the carpenter's shop - until the time, that is, that it began to get in the way of the motor-cars.

It stood square across the way facing the whole length of the street and obliged the roadway to split into two immediately in front of the double doors of the rough-boarded, timber building and pass on either side.

The roads joined again at a point some 50 yards further on, having created an island that became known as Potter's Green. It was an island that could only have existed up to the end of the 1920s and had the charm of unplanned expediency.

There was not only Potter's woodworking shed on the piece of ground, but it was backed by a lean-to forge and a wheelwright's yard and space enough left for a stretch of grass and a couple of pollarded trees.

Beneath these the regulars from the Dragon across the way would often sit on the bench and sip their beer, feeling that they were in the midst of all that was going on.

So they were. On fine days the carpenter's shop spilled out into the open with its heartening sounds of hammer and saw, and with the growing construction of gates and coffins and window frames. At the rear, the smith was always busy with horses waiting to be shod or fixing an iron tyre on to a waggon wheel.

They were sights familiar enough but always worth watching. What with these activities on Potter's Green and the fact that all travellers to or from the village would pass or linger at the spot, it was obvious that there was not much in the rural world that was not going on just there.

Potter himself was a competent tradesman who had been an estate carpenter and later set up on his own, by nature an unctuous, narrow man, careful to keep on the right side of the village, of the gentry, and if possible, of heaven itself.

There were two apprentices indentured for seven years and Potter's only son, Percy, who was considered to be soft in the head. He worked on simple jobs in the shed but feared to go far and seldom ventured out of his father's sight.

"I dussen't go abroad very far", he would tell you with open simplicity. "I'm better at hoom. O' course, I'm a crorss to father." This was something he was quite sure about, having been told so often. "I'm a proper crorss to bear, I am".

It was a cross that the senior Potter made a good deal of. Yet, apart from the schoolboys who sometimes came down to the Green to pelt him with conkers, Percy had a good deal of sympathy from the villagers and at least one fast friend.

This was the boy who helped the smith at the adjacent forge. His name was Brewster and he was a Dr. Barnado boy. Something in his nature or in his experience made him resent the job which many boys would have given almost anything to do, and he worked the bellows and watched the fire as if it were

104

the flames of hell itself. He showed the same ferocity in chasing off the boys who came to bait Percy and an odd kind of understanding existed between the two.

There were two other regulars on the Green. These were the two old men who sat under the tree in the fine weather and regarded the carpenter's shop with something of proprietorial interest. Inside were their own coffins, made to their own careful specifications and resting in the store-room at the back.

Both old men had satisfied themselves that the coffins were of high quality and would accommodate them snugly when required.

These were the characters of the Green some 50 years ago and each played a part in the mystery that some local people still remember.

It occurred one August in the early 1920s.

Perhaps it was that the concentration of interests on the tiny Green had become too much for such a tiny area.

Perhaps the days for such rough and ready enterprises were already over and it needed very little to unbalance the whole arrangement and bring it to an end. Nobody dreamed, however, that the end would be quite so sudden.

The moment of unbalance began when a new element arrived and added its encumbrances to the Green. It was in the shape of gaily coloured cart covered with canvas hood and drawn by one lean horse.

It arrived one Saturday morning before the Dragon was open and drew up on the Green. From the cart a gipsy-like couple produced the equipment for a stall and a mass of cheapjack wares.

Throughout the day the stall attracted a changing group of villagers who came as much for the fun and excitement of listening to the cheapjack's "gift of the gab" as for anything else. Many found a need, however, to buy a little bottle of the elixir offered for sale since few of them could claim to be free of every one of the complaints it promised to cure.

Less certain were they of newly-miraculous cleaning materials or of the articles of dress brought directly from the centres of fashion. The Dragon's customers stayed to look, as did the apprentices to whom Saturday was a work-day until noon: Brewster seemed to be fascinated and spent much of his time eyeing the stall but Percy merely peered out from the shadows of the carpenter's shop and came no nearer.

Nor did the old men on the bench, for they could see all that they wanted and were past hoping that bottles of physic would renew their old bones.

In the afternoon the Potter's shed was closed and locked and the fire in the smithy allowed to go down, but there was a good deal of activity around the stall until late evening when the gipsies closed up and repaired to the Dragon.

In the small hours of the morning the landlord of the Dragon awoke with a sense of noise and violence in the air. The carpenter's shop on the Green was ablaze and burning like a torch.

The roar and crackle of the flames was rousing other people nearby and they turned out into the street to watch with awe the indomitable power of a fire on dry match-boarding and piles of timber.

There was little that could be done, though the fire-pump was brought from the church hall and a

106

chain of men handed buckets of water from the pond. It was just impossible to get near the blaze.

Daylight saw the complete destruction of the Potter's shed, of finished gates and window frames and the two coffins belonging to the old men, while the smithy was a smouldering mound of bricks.

So far as could be seen no one was hurt or caught in the fires but there was a great deal about the catastrophe that needed to be questioned.

For one thing, Percy had been seen at the height of the fire apparently fully dressed and walking up and down as if distraught, although the senior Potter did not appear until later.

Moreover, the travelling cheap-jacks had packed and gone in a hurry and young Brewster was nowhere to be found.

Few people doubted that someone must have set fire to the building and there were many, including his own apprentices, who had some score to pay against Potter.

But the immediate mystery was that of Brewster's disappearance and a further search was made of the debris in case he had been caught in the inferno after all. In time people came to the opinion, which seems to be correct, that Brewster had gone off with the cheap-jacks who pushed off quickly for that reason and that Percy had set fire to the shed in sheer despair after Brewster had come to bid him goodbye.

For a time the charred debris littered the Green, but the times were gone when such places could ever be built again.

The piece was eventually cleared and made level and a substantial slice taken away to improve the road.

In a few months there was no sign or vestige remaining of Potter's Green except that Percy would come and stand there forlornly from time to time as if waiting for Brewster to come back.

Randy Moss

In the earliest part of the morning, before the sun came down the cottage roofs and splashed light on the small windows and into the dew-wet gardens, young Randy Moss came forth to find a job.

He was just 13, and having no coat against the chill of the morning, ran all the way from his cottage door as far as the Ettram Mill. There, he stood on the threshold of the great mill house and held his hat awkwardly in the bird-sharp stillness.

There were two sizeable steps to the door and Randy placed a foot on each as if equally in mind to advance or retreat.

He tugged at his collarless shirt and brushed his nose with the bunched-up hat before ever he dared to knock and not for a second did he take his eyes from the crack of the door.

There was a subdued shouting and steps inside.

"Not Jilly," he thought, "surely not Jilly."

It was Jilly, soft and sleepy from bed; Jilly en deshabille, luxurious with being loved and cared for, and only 12 years old.

"Tha's on'y me, Jilly - miss." He wrung his hat desperately. "That was your father I wanted to ask . . . ."

"That you, Randy?" she said in sleepy surprise. Her mother came up behind her and Jilly disappeared. Suddenly the miller was there: his face was lined and twisted with suspicion. He fought the world with suspicion, Randy thought, to keep – perhaps to keep Jilly safe and warm in bed.

"Mornin', master," Randy began hoarsely. 'I'm on'y Randy Moss from down the village an' I a'come to ask ef yew ha' got a job." The miller only stared. "I'm fairly strong," Randy said. "I ain't afraid o' work."

The miller stared relinquishing nothing of his suspicion but mindful of his breakfast. "Dew yew go along into the mill - I'll see yew presently."

Randy scuttled into the mill and waited. Tha's jest easy gittin' a job, he thought, tha's jest easy. Three shillings he'd ask for wages, and all but sixpence he'd give to his mother. He wanted the day to go quickly, so that he could tell her.

Jilly came into the mill during the morning. She was sharp, now, and pert, not like the sleepy doll he had seen earlier.

"Lift that bag up for me Randy. Lift it, stupid. And that one." He piled the sacks up at her bidding and she sat there delicately like a queen.

Randy worked on the concrete floor and he had no tiredness feeling the warmth of her just sitting there, she and her strange and tender daintiness in the rough mill.

There was no telling of the time, but he reckoned he had shovelled corn for three or four hours when she suddenly disappeared and he dared to rest nervously, tying rags about the red blisters on his hands.

When she came back she was eating and she gave him a piece of gingerbread. Still he dared not stop lest the miller looked in, and he all but choked on the morsel.

"Would you like to get my ribbon?" she asked teasingly. The pink ribbon came from her hair and floated like some exotic antenna as she held one end and threw the other towards him.

Time and again the ribbon streamed out and was furled up again. In the end he tried to grab it and they laughed at her quickness.

Once he caught it but she jerked it out of his hands and held it behind her back.

"Next time," he shouted, and flung himself upon the prize. She squealed and struggled to collect the ribbon but he held on until it slipped from his fingers and she hid it behind her back. He was laughing and feeling behind her for the ribbon with her golden hair in his face and her strong limbs pushing him away.

"You didn't - " she was screaming and the words came momentarily after the laughter had gone and they were apart and frightened with the miller standing over them.

Whatever he was shouting was lost in the staggering clout that landed on Randy's ear and deafened him. He tried to run away and saw Jilly slipping out of the mêlée for the safety of her mother's apron as he tripped and stumbled among the corn sacks.

He felt himself pulled up and pushed headlong into the small shed where the samples of grain were kept. The door was slammed violently and locked.

Shaken and frightened, Randy listened and waited, knowing that in a moment he had lost his job and the day's wages and Jilly.

Worse still, he faced what frightful confrontation

with the miller when the door was eventually unlocked! He was bruised and aching with the events of the morning and his head sang.

Judging by the sun, dropping past the small, cobwebbed window, he guessed it to be nearly three o' clock in the afternoon when the sound of slight and hesitant footsteps came into the mill.

Suddenly the door was opened and Jilly was there, red-eyed, hand still on the bolt and shaking with fright.

"You better go - quick", she whispered.

The boy ran, squirming out of the mill like a frightened rabbit. Jilly followed too, to the boundary fence, but Randy was running as he had never run before - until he knew that there was no pursuit and then he pulled up under a hedgebank to recover his breath.

One thing was certain - he dared not go home; not because he feared a beating from his father, but because he would be ashamed to tell his mother that he had gained and lost a job in the same day.

By four o' clock Randy had reached Gant's farm on the other side of the village. Podgy Gant saw him plodding up to the farm along the cart track. Podgy was a pig farmer; there were pens of shrieking pigs in the buildings and a morass of mud outside.

"A job?" he said. "Tha's a rum time o' the day to come arter a job. But I can give you a job if you ain't afraid of pigs. How much do you want?"

"Three shillings - or half-a-crown," Randy wavered.

"Well," said Podgy dryly, "I reckon that'll be half-a-crown. But I shan't pay you for what you do today."

112

Randy worked until six, carrying pails of food into the pig pens, too tired and desperate to be afraid, though twice he was pushed over into the muck and once momentarily crushed by an old sow against the fence.

Randy got back to the cottage and faced his mother.

"I got a job, mum. I got a job."

He was surprised when his mother looked in his face and saw the scars and cried.

The Last Threshing

"Yew did say," Tom greeted me one morning as I came into the yard, "as yew was a-going to milk Daisy. Well - tha's done. I done har afore I started."

There was more to come. "I reckon yew'll find all yew want to dew down 'ere at the gate," Tom continued with heavy satisfaction. "The throshin' tackle 'a' come, tha's half in half out o' the gate and can't git one way nor yit t'other."

"But it's not due until tomorrow," I protested.

"Ah, yes," Tom patiently allowed for the ignorance of young farmers. "But d'y'see they atter come afore the day for the settin'in. Dew they'd be all them min a-standin' around tomorrow waiting to begin."

Instead of waiting around today, I thought, looking at the total strength of four farm men and five threshing tackle followers all closely considering the situation at the gate and apparently willing it to right itself.

The tackle was of the kind that still moved from farm to farm right up to the end of the last war. There was the steam traction engine, already through the gate and chuffing and hissing steam all over the polished brass, the threshing drum behind it leaning doubtfully against one of the gateposts and in the rear the elevator sticking uselessly out into the middle of the road.

114

The traction engine driver was obviously doubtful about any further manoeuvres to free the drum and was relieved when I set the men to dig out the post. Then, with a shudder and a clatter the contraption shook itself into motion and eased into the drive. An elderly, cheerless-looking man in a long mac belted with string followed close beside until the procession came to a halt again beside the stackyard.

The engine driver, a local contractor named George Chapman, wiped his hands and jumped down beside the man in the mac.

"How dew she sound, Charlie?" he asked. "She fare to me to be a-wheezin' a trifle."

Charlie looked despondently at the engine. "The way yew use har tha's a wonder she don't blow harself up."

The two men listened again and then began the task of "setting-in" in the stackyard. The careful disposition of the engine, level and true for the tension of the driving belt, the placing of coal and water nearby, the arrangement of the elevator and the checking of the thresher took them all of the next three hours. Then there was the statutory wire-netting to be put round the site in order to capture the rats.

The year was 1945 and another war-time regulation was that stacks should be no less than a certain distance apart. This sometimes caused farmers to make stacks of excessive size - this stack was as big as a barn. Three would be needed - two Land Army girls and a man - on that cornstack and a further two men on the straw. Young Brian would look to the rats and Fred to the carting. Three more men would be required on the drum, with Tom at the corn chute, one on the chaff and another as the 'bin-cutter'. I hastily tallied up the manpower in case I was landed with the unwholesome chaff chute and found that all would be well. Charlie, from long experience, would be bin-cutter.

"He's done that job" George Chapman told me, "ever since I began 12 years ago, an' I never knew anyone whu could dew the job better. But he's a funny bloke - never work for anyone regular. He's follered this tackle, come fair or foul, everywhere I 'a'bin. I don't ever ask him - I jest set off with the tackle for some farm an' I find he's a follerin' on behind or he's there afore I am. I pay him for the hours he dew - an' as sune as the job is over he's gone. Poor owd Charlie. What he'll dew arter this I don't know."

George Chapman, I learned, was about to give up his threshing business. Already, with the war over, the tackle was an anachronism. Farmers could drive a thresher from their own tractors and were ordering balers instead of elevators. This job was the last before the engine, tackle and George himself retired.

Next morning the two Land Army girls arrived in a War Ag. van and soon afterwards, the whole paraphernalia of threshing tackle was in humming motion, even the traction engine slightly rocking as it panted and sweated to keep the belt turning. There was something fascinating, both in the music of the operation and in the activity - a pleasant and satisfying collaboration of nature, humanity and mechanical ingenuity. King over all was Charlie on the roof of the drum, a different and a more confident Charlie than the one I had seen hitherto.

Without his mac, arms bare and knife in hand, he stood over the snarling mouth of the thresher and fed the sheaves in swiftly and regularly. In this situation, speeding the bottle-neck of the proceedings, his stature and strength were those of a giant. Despite the three on the corn stack he picked up each sheaf as it arrived, swung and cut the string and was back for another in surprisingly swift, graceful movements.

At bait time he came and stood beside the engine to eat his bread and cheese, looking and listening.

George Chapman shouted: "She sound all right today, Charlie bor. She's properly a-singing." Charlie looked up and grinned: - "Properly a-singing", he said.

But when all was over and the great corn stack had passed every straw through the drum Charlie put on his mac again and his former dispirited air. He began to walk away down the drive.

George Chapman set the tackle in motion once more for the last journey home. When he got opposite to Charlie he shouted:

"Cor, she di'n't half sing today, Charlie. She sung di'n't she?"

Charlie looked his last on the thing he had loved as it passed him and said with an effort:

"Yeah, she sung. She wholly sung."

Martha and the Tree

The new boy at the farm came singing to work every morning. We turned our mouths down when we heard him. He wouldn't last long. Nobody could sing and do farm work - that was a serious business. But he kept singing.

He sang the songs he had learned at school in a treble voice that was beginning to break and he poured the notes down into the dull soil as he bent over his tasks. When he raised his head the clear voice came floating upwards - like a lark he sang with abandon into the free air, but like a lark dipped his voice when he turned back to the earth.

He sang for as long as his small body could stand the labour and all the extra labour heaped upon him simply because he sang. He sang for six weeks before his spirit broke and he became silent and then the silence was complete.

From then on he neither sang nor spoke and worked with a sullenness that accompanied him all through the day and followed him as he left the yard at night.

He's settled down, we said - we'll make a man of him yet. Though how he kept singing for so long . . .

Someone said, "That was a rare voice, though. Owd Martha, she used to come outta har cottage every day a listenin' at the bottom o' her garden."

"Oh, Martha - she's crazy. But that was funny, somehow, how he could fare to work an' sing at the same time. I ha' never heard anybody else dew that. Even that day when we tried to make him stop, d'yew remember? He was a cleanin' out the ditch an' we tol' him the boss was a-watching an' if he stop work for a second he'd git the sack. That nearly bruk his back. He still kep' singin' but he was a-cryin' tew."

Ah well, we all atter grow up, we said. But we shook our heads over the boy. He's a rum boy, we said. He ain't one o' us.

Old Martha, the queer old woman from the cottages, came to the fence every day to listen, but there was no more singing. Whenever one of the farm men came within reach of her shrill voice she would go on about the boy. "What ha' yew done wi' that poor boy?" she would say. "Yew togither, yew ha' done away wi' him."

The men would laugh and point to the boy working off somewhere on his own. "There he is - he don't look dead to me!" They laughed at their own wit but the old woman took no notice. "Yew ha' buried him," she shrieked.

Nobody ever bothered about what Martha said, for it was known that she was half mad, yet the idea stuck in my mind that there was some truth in what she said, for I had been with the boy when he had stopped singing.

I was working behind him in that ditch in which he had sung and cried together. It was heavy work and I could see he had trouble in carrying on. His singing seemed to falter and in the middle of a line the life went out of him.

He folded up, leaning on his spade as if he had no

119

strength left, as if he were an old man. He rested for five minutes and then began to work again but I never heard him sing after that day.

A month later the boy left the farm and no one knew where he went. It must have been two or three years before the ditch got cleaned out again. The undergrowth had grown quite a lot and there was even a substantial sapling growing on the field side of the ditch; a young ash.

As the men worked in the ditch they were astonished to see old Martha come through a gap in the hedge from time to time and go to the tree. Once when they looked there was a bundle of feathers, a sloughed snake's skin and a small doll placed there. "Don't yew touch that tree," the old woman would shrill. "I ha' put my mark on that tree. Tha's where that poor boy is buried."

Perhaps I should have treated the old woman with the contempt of the farm men but there was something faintly credible in the fancy that the whispering leaves of the young ash tree was some sort of living projection of the boy's lost voice. We'll leave the tree, I thought; it won't be in the way.

But when the ditchers got to that spot old Martha was there in a screaming fit, woe-betide-ing any who were rash enough to touch the sapling. In irritation, one of the men slashed the stem about half-way up, almost severing it. "Well, I ain't dead yit," he said, getting back into the ditch.

But he was - almost completely dead. For the disease inside him was close to domination, and he came no more to the farm after the spring. It was one of those coincidences that sometimes happen, and I knew that you could always link events with warnings and forebodings if you took the trouble and had the inclination to do so. In this case the idea of cause and effect was ridiculous, even to the farm men.

The sapling, now five or six feet high, appeared to heal with a miraculous speed. The old witch had put on splints and sacking over the gash and in a few weeks the cambium had grown together and the tree was thriving again.

You could often see the old woman there walking with her shawl over her bent shoulders or searching the ground for whatever her old head was seeking. People left her alone because she was fierce and unpleasant and it seemed safer to keep out of her way.

Certainly I always avoided her, perhaps from some deep-laid superstition about the evil eye or suchlike, but it became clear that it was towards me that her malevolence was chiefly directed. She would confront me suddenly in the lane, in the fields or even in the stackyard, standing there and staring as I went past, not saying a single word as far as I could hear but making me feel far less than comfortable.

She was becoming a nuisance. I had no reason to go out of my way to destroy the tree, but if she insisted on these confrontations then I would get rid of it once and for all. The opportunity came when we took delivery of our first power-mounted plough, for seeing how it swung out over the ditches at the headlands it seemed that I could now reasonably condemn the ash for being in the way.

At the end of the harvest that year I stayed on the farm while my wife with the three children went off on a fortnight's holiday in the Yorkshire dales. Perhaps it was a kind of superstition again but I would not touch the tree until they were well away from the farm - just in case.

Then I took a spade along the edge of the field and dug the ash up, lifting its roots and all out of the ground, and took it gingerly back to the farmyard.

Nothing happened, except that I saw old Martha come to the spot where the tree had been and later I saw her nearer to the farmhouse staring in at the windows. It was a bit of nonsense finished with, I hoped.

Next day, I heard that my wife had had a minor accident in the car. Nobody was seriously hurt but my wife had a lacerated arm. How did it happen, I wanted to know? No one seemed to know. There had been no collision with another vehicle and my wife was driving in quite a happy and relaxed way.

In fact, they said, she was singing.

I went into the yard in time to see Martha taking away the tree.

It was still whole except for the arm-like branch that hung down, and I was suddenly devoutly thankful that I had done no other damage — or destroyed the tree utterly.

Martha took the tree and planted it in her own garden. In the years since, it has grown very tall.

I don't know if it sings. I never stay long enough to find out.

Tickler Tom

T he old man we used to know as Tickler or Tom
Tickler carried this odd nickname throughout
his life for no other reason than that it was his
father's.

He was a simple and unimpressive man whose filial
loyalties and childhood memories caused him to
treasure the fact that, like his father, he too was
Tickler Tom. To him it was a continued symbol of his
father's almost legendary reputation as ploughman
and local character - a kind of reflected glow in which
he bathed, perhaps excessively, when daily realities
began to fade.

He would often tell the stories of his father's life as
he believed them to be true but in his dotage his
memory began to play tricks and he would ramble on
among the half-forgotten tracks that were misty with
time.

Yet in the ramblings only the facts suffered: what
came from them all the clearer was the composite
impression of country life long ago, before his own
lifetime and even before his father's.

"Course, that was long afore my time," the old man
would say doubtfully, as if he knew it to be true but
could scarcely believe it himself - "long afore my time
when they took the wool away 'cos of the new
machines.

"So stid o' wool, the folk round about here, well
they tunned to what they call hemp. Yeah, thas right,

hemp."

He would look at you as if he could hardly expect you to believe it either in an age when you had to travel miles to find a single break-crop from sugar-beet and corn, but he would go on, nevertheless, to describe how important the hemp crop had once been to Suffolk. A great fertile stretch of the county north and east of Eye had been used almost entirely for this crop and as the wool trade died out the local skills were used in the processing of hemp.

All was done by specialised work in the villages from the retting in pits of water to the spinning and weaving - for the hemp hereabouts was so fine that it was made into cloth and used for garments, its quality comparable with that of linen. Nowhere else in the world could such fibre be produced.

Tickler Tom's grandmother, before ever she bore the boy who was to become the original Tickler, was somehow occupied with the hemp. From her skill she spun and wove the fibre for garments for her own husband's back, buying the tow from the local huckster and disdaining the services of the whitester since she reckoned that the stuff would last longer if it were in the natural brown.

Her husband wore them - shirts and jacket alike in rough brown hemp - until he died and they were handed with a handful of possessions to his eldest son, the original Tickler. He it was who continued to wear the garments and was given the nickname by village folk who had long given up hemp for such up-to-date material as flannel.

Tickler Tom the first, however, was an individualist, a man whose growing stature in the village allowed him not merely to ignore the rustic raillery but to make a point of wearing the garments whenever he appeared at ploughing matches.

He became a "character," but not to laugh at: the hempen shirts identified and placed him and such was his reputation that the rough hemp became a thing for admiration.

Tickler had other advantages beside his skill and his lonely, determined nature, for his employer was a landowner-farmer who was not only tolerant of Tickler's ploughing career but kept the best horses and ploughs in the area. When the new and revolutionary Ransomes YL plough came out he was the first to use it.

With it, Tickler was able to astonish the neighbouring small farmers with a new facility and accuracy, until it was decreed in many of the local ploughing matches that ploughs must be of the standard type and until more farmers used the new YL then the competitions must be confined to the old wooden beam plough.

It made but little difference to Tickler. If it were to be a beam plough then he would win with a beam plough: if it had to be a two horse team or a three-horse team he would win. On one occasion he won even with a team of oxen.

Tickler would take on all comers and never disdained the small village meetings. Tickler came twice to the village of Tarlton to take part in the competitions. At that time he was about 30 years old and had not yet acquired the status that later allowed him to travel into distant counties for more important prizes. Yet even these two meetings were talked of by the villagers for years afterwards.

At the first he won the pair of buskins that the landlord of the Swan had offered and at the second he yielded his place in order to win a greater prize . . . . .

It was on a late October day that Tickler brought over his plough in the farm wagon together with his favourite pair of horses. About six teams were taking part that day and the field was nice and convenient - opposite the Swan and running alongside the open green.

Tickler measured his stetch and put in new-peeled sticks, then carefully set up the plough and harnessed up. Already his reputation had gone before him and oldsters and apprentice hands gathered to watch the work of the hempen wonder.

The crowd kept Molly, the girl at the Swan, busy with the carrying of tankards across the road and into the stubble field, for no one waited for beer until the contest finished. Tickler himself called for a tankard as he finished his first round and waited until Molly had brought it to him. For Tickler only one thing could properly be attended to at a time, and he laid the guiding lines on the plough handles as he watched the girl bring the heavy tankards over the rough stubble and watched her go back and watched her come again. With his tankard full, she stood beside him for a moment, as lively as the autumn breeze.

"Yew reckon yew'll win?" she asked casually. Tickler found himself wishing that it were important to her - to involve her in his success.

"Dew yew want me to win?" he countered.

She tossed her head. "It don't matter what I want. I reckon yew'll win anyway." She gathered up some glasses and more orders and went off back to the inn.

Refreshed, Tickler continued with his ploughing, the prize being for the best workmanlike stetch of nine feet and showing straight furrows and a neat flag. With only one last furrow to draw he called again for ale and waited for Molly to bring it. He had made up his mind how he could prove himself to her.

She came up and said: "They reckon you're as good as won, a 'riddy." He shook his head. "That depend on you. I can win - but ef you was to ask me to lose, well, I'd lose ef you wanted me to."

She drew back. "I don't want you to lose - not for me."

"But ef I did, jist for you, that'd show that matter to me what you think, wou'n't it?"

Suddenly realising the implications of the proposed sacrifice, Molly flushed and hesitated. "You woun't dare," she said.

But Tickler would.

He lifted her without a word on to the back of the nearside horse and she sat there laughing and squealing as the last furrow became a triumphant procession and no account given to any prize but Molly.

Everyone cheered and somehow it all added to Tickler's fame. When he married her a few weeks afterwards the whole neighbourhood turned out for the wedding.

Ivy

It had been a disappointing morning for the peapickers - nine o' clock before the sun came through to drive away the damp mists, then another half hour before the foreman shouted from the trailer: "Come and get your bags!"

In an instant the motley gathering of pickers lost its depression and made beelines for the trailer packed with hessian sacks. They snatched at the bundles of sacks and carried them off quickly to the edge of the field where the rows began.

Some of the pickers ran - a couple holding a bag between them, a gaunt old man on his own, women from the village in aprons and gumboots, a group of gipsies already arguing about the price, all of them aware that speed had become urgent.

Ahead of them all, of course, was Ivy, for no one ever beat Ivy to the picking. Already she was bent double over the rows.

Ivy was the complete professional picker, not like the other village women who worked only at their own convenience. In turn she picked strawberries and blackcurrants, peas and potatoes.

Whatever and wherever it was, Ivy was the first to know and the first to pick, often trundling her bike along the lanes before daylight with her pail clanking against the handlebars and her gumboots slung round her neck. For Ivy, who lived quietly and alone during the darker months of the year, the short picking season was something to prepare for and fight through as though it were a battle campaign.

While she picked, Ivy turned an anxious eye on the growing number of newcomers. The field would not last the day, she thought. It was always the same; no matter how early you came the word got around and people flocked to the field. All you could do was to pick faster and faster to make sure of your share before it ended. At 1s. 3d. for a 40lb bag it would be a fair day if it lasted until three o' clock and she could show six full bags.

As the sun became stronger, Ivy led the line of scattered pickers down the field, a familiar figure in her old black, wide brimmed hat and protective aprons.

The hessian sack became steadily fuller and heavy to pull along and she began picking into the handier pail. She was conscious that there was someone working close behind her but she was too busy to look round. At 11 o'clock the alarm clock boomed off inside her basket and she slumped down immediately on a pile of pea haulm and ate her thick sandwiches.

Ivy spared herself only five minutes for the break, but it was long enough for a stretch and a gaze around.

Close behind the pickers were the farm men with the trailer, the foreman carrying his bag of bright new shillings from the bank but with his eyes on everything before he handed them out. When he came to any full bags, the foreman would bounce them up and down to make sure they were of the weight required then thrust his hand down the inside of the sack.

If he were satisfied, he would hand the money to the picker while another man tied the sack with binder twine and threw it on the trailer. It was an apparently

129

casual but efficient operation provided the men worked close together and kept their eyes on the sacks.

They were not always quick enough for the gippos, thought Ivy. They work together and have perhaps ten sacks ready to be tied. With the gippos milling around and the foreman counting the money it was often possible for one of them to pull back a sack that had been tied, cut the string and have it paid for again.

The gippos, Ivy knew, were up to all sorts of tricks. Like filling the bottom of the sack with haulm and clods to make weight. But, of course, a foreman with his wits about him soon learned to deal with that, and many a bag was tipped out on to the ground without ceremony. Better to be honest, thought Ivy. Better to have an easy conscience.

When she got back to the picking she found that her neighbour, the tall, gaunt man had already overtaken her. It was a challenge Ivy had to meet.

The man smiled when he heard the alarm and decided that he would have a break too. He made a big heap of the haulm they had pulled up and they sat together against the soft coolness of the leaves. Now that he could relax, the man spoke for the first time, offering Ivy tea from his flask.

"Tha's a masterpiece," he was saying, "yew a-catchin' up wi' me. I ain't ever known any one else whew c'd dew that. Fact, I thought yew was a-goin' to leave me behind there, once. No doubt about ut, ma'am, yew an' me, we ought to be partners."

Ivy ate her sandwiches consideringly. "How'd yew mean, partners?"

"I mean, jest for the pickin', like. I don't suggest no more, ma'am. I reckon yew ha' a'riddy got some man

130

a-dotin' on yew."

"No, I hain't, said Ivy indignantly. "An' I don't want one."

"We c'd help each other, dew yew see?" the gaunt man went on. "Look at them hands." He took one of her hands and turned it over. It was black with the pea haulm. She was half pleased, half ashamed.

"They ain't allust like that," she said, like a young girl.

"I'll lay they ain't. I'll lay yew -" but he decided not to pursue this line of thought. He looked round at the approaching trailer. "Now, partner, how'd yew like another bag o' peas quick? Ef yew was to go an' hev a word wi' that foreman there, jest keep him talkin' for a minute-".

Ivy looked at the man, her heart sinking with disappointment, but she went. She spoke to the foreman and both he and the other man were engrossed in what she was saying. During that time, Ivy's partner had slid round to the blind side of the trailer and pulled off two bags, cutting the twine as he hauled them back to add to their pile of full bags.

"There y'are," he gloated. "Another bag for me an' one for yew, partner."

"No, I can't take them," Ivy protested. "That ain't right."

The gaunt man looked at her consideringly. "Well, I understand," he said. "Tha's womanly conscience. That dew yew credit, ma'am. But we're still partners, ain't we?"

By now the groups of pickers were converging on the remaining area of unpicked peas. The field would be finished even earlier than Ivy had thought.

Ivy felt disappointed and heavy-hearted. When the trailer came close she sat with her back to the field, hidden by the haulm. It was no good hoping, she thought; he would take the money for all their bags and disappear.

Some partnership - but you had to hope while you could.

After ten minutes, she looked round. The bags had gone and so had the man. Stupid as it was, she could not help feeling more disappointed at the man's weakness than with the loss of the money.

She was gathering her belongings into her bag when she heard his voice behind her.

"I've brought yar bike," he said. "So you can pack yar things on. An' here's yar share o' the money. I didn't take any for them tew bags I got - yew reckoned that was wrong. I thought 'haps we could ride a bit o' the way along the rood togither."

Jimmy and the German

Jimmy Bird looked at the sky in the morning and thought that there would be no rain. The sun was scudding through light summer clouds and for a time the clouds foamed around the sun and veiled its brilliance then disgorged it utterly into a clear blue sky and disappeared. It was going to be another bright, clear September day.

Despite the air-raids, Jimmy loved these days of the Indian summer. The land was still, as if passion-spent and satisfied, free of the demands of the rest of the year. Bonus days, he thought, a respite before the cycle began again. Except, of course, for the air raids.

Jimmy was clearing the ditches on Umberstone Farm. In the morning he had already done the ditch on the road side of Whippletree Field and the rubbish lay piled in heaps on the lip of the ditch.

It was mostly young growth of blackthorn and hazel with grass and patches of bracken and nettle - good material for bonfires. There were six heaps to be burned and more to be raked out of the ditch and a useful bundle of pea-sticks to take home on his bicycle at the end of the day.

He thought that he would light the fires early because by war-time regulations they must be out by dusk and he had barely set light to the fires when the siren started. Jimmy went on combing the ditch and looking up at the clear sky when he could hear aeroplane engines but there was not much to see up there as yet.

The procedure now, he knew, was for German bombers to come over in a mass, escorted by fighters that swarmed like metallic gnats high up against the roof of the sky. The days of impudent, low-level attacks like the one he had seen take place over Martlesham aerodrome were over.

In those earlier raids he had watched the swastikas dive to the target and release the pairs of bombs that writhed and swirled in the air before they struck the ground. It was spectacular, but somehow not so menacing as these massed raids at high altitude.

When the AA guns began, Jimmy looked up again to distinguish the puffs of smoke. Around him from time to time the silence was shattered by racing Spitfires as they hedge-hopped from nearby air-fields in their anxiety to get to the fray, but little else was visible and only the growing crescendo of noise from hundreds of engines told him that the considerable armada was passing over some miles to the north.

He had been working for some time in the bottom of the ditch clearing around the exit of a drain with his stick and bagging iron when he happened to look across the field.

There was a man there. He was walking diagonally across the stubble as if heading for the farm buildings but when he caught sight of the two bomb craters left after an earlier raid he turned aside, looked down into one of them for a few seconds and then slid down out of sight.

Jimmy's heart was pounding: it was a German airman he had no doubt. What he did have doubts about was what he was expected to do in such a situation and his first instinct was to go on working as if nothing had happened.

Recent training at the village Home Guard centre, however, did not agree with this easy way out. After all, wasn't that really what the Home Guard was for - to trap and capture enemy parachutists?

Jimmy desperately tried to remember something about capturing Germans and unarmed combat but he was a peaceful man and had mentally rejected such confrontation. All he could remember was the idea of demoralising the enemy first with an aggressive shout.

Jimmy was not good at shouting either. He wished he had never seen the airman or that he would climb out of the hole and go away. He felt sick in the stomach and could not go on working. He would have to face it - confront the enemy and demoralise him with a great shout and a flourish of the bagging iron.

He began to walk across to the craters, his feeling of inadequacy increased by the thought that perhaps he should be crawling or running or making a reccy. His sergeant was very fond of a reccy.

At a point about 30 yards from the crater Jimmy began to run or at least to stumble through the stubble and began to shout "Yaryaryar" in a rather unfrightening sort of voice.

When he got to the crater he jumped in with a further yell and landed awkwardly. "Oh Christ!" he said and all but forgot the German as he felt the pain from his ankle shoot up his leg. He sat there for a minute groaning and looking down at his foot. The German, he could see through the cloud of pain, was leaning against the side of the hole smoking a cigarette.

At least there was no need for unarmed combat, even

135

if he could have attempted it, he thought, but he must take the initiative. He picked up the bagging iron and pointed it at the Nazi, who had the trappings of a high-ranking officer.

"Don't yew move, now," Jimmy said. "I'm a takin' yew prisoner. Dew yew keep stiddy now. Ooh, blast this ankle!"

The German, who had viewed Jimmy's arrival without much concern, said politely in clear English:

"I shall help you? You smoke?"

Jimmy gave up trying to follow the canons of military procedures. "That soddin' hole," he groaned, taking the cigarette. "I forgot that was as deep as that." He tried to move his foot and the German bent down and unlaced the boot and looked at the swelling ankle.

"A sprain, I would think," he said, "Perhaps some cold water . . . ."

"I ain't got no cowd water - on'y cowd tea, in my bag over there."

"I shall get it for you."

"No, yew don't" he said. "You're my prisoner. That don't fare right lettin' yew git away."

"Get away?" echoed the German. "Where to should I get away? I tell you my friend I am happy to be your prisoner and I have every intention to staying with you. I have no wish to risk violence from the village people." While he was gone Jimmy rubbed his ankle and tried to assess the situation. There seemed to be only two alternatives - to wait in the crater for a time hoping that the ankle would improve after a rest, or to ask his prisoner to help him out of the crater and support him along the village street to his home. The latter was unthinkable - they would have to wait.

136

The German came back with Jimmy's lunch bag and they shared the sandwiches and some of the cold tea. The rest they poured over a handkerchief and tied it round the ankle. Jimmy tried to stand but slithered over in the clay. He sat there for a long time and the German became impatient.

"You know it is your responsibility to hand me over to the proper authorities - or shall we wait and starve, perhaps, while your foot is healing? Come, let me help you to your home and end this nonsense."

Jimmy shook his head. The prisoner turned suddenly to his pack and produced a pistol used for firng flares. "Take this," he said, "and point it at my head. Everyone will think I am helping you under the threat of death. Good?"

It was very good, Jimmy thought, but still physically difficult to achieve.

It was after he remembered the wheelbarrow in the nearby barn that the idea became perfect. A small boy picking blackberries saw them first and ran to tell the village people. Everyone gathered to see Jimmy, apparently wounded, forcing the Nazi to trundle him home in a wheelbarrow, and wondered at his courage.

At his own door Jimmy was helped in by willing hands. He waved the gun towards the German and said, "Now you're here yew better come in for a cup o' tea."

The sentence made the headlines in the hero-hungry newspapers next morning.

Courting Strong

After tea on Tuesday, July 19, 1929, the little country station went to sleep as usual until about seven o'clock. The evening sunlight mellowed the station buildings and picked out long shadows on the gravel in front of the deserted booking-office.

At half past six the quiet was scarcely broken when George Palmer brought his pony and trap into the yard and pulled up by the fence. The pony nibbled the hedge and shook its bridle chains impatiently, but George sat and waited on the board seat of the trap until the train came in.

As the engine hissed and fussed beside the platform, half-a-dozen passengers appeared - among them a plump, middle-aged woman carrying a parcel.

George saw her and waited until she came and stood beside him. He thought she would show her disappointment when she saw his grey hair and old, slumped body, but she was smiling.

"Hullo, George," she said, as if it had not been 30 years since they had last spoken together. For a moment they looked at each other, then he reached out a hand and pulled her up to the seat beside him.

"I thought you was dead, George," she said wonderingly.

"Not yit, I ain't" he assured her, a bit put out at the idea.

"I mean - afore you writ that letter. That seemed sech a long time since I had heard from you, I thought I shou'n't ever see you agen, George." She put her hand over his and he smiled.

"Wonders never cease," he said almost gaily, and shook the reins. She smiled too. "Take me hoom, George," she said.

The romance had begun nearly 30 years before. George, and all the other Palmers, lived in the rambling old cottage that stood without much confidence well back from the road. They were a large family even by standards then, and there were frequent difficulties in the feeding of 12 mouths every day around the kitchen table.

Once a year, in the autumn, George's father would kill one of his own pigs for themselves and for weeks afterwards the house would be full of the business of salting and curing, cutting and hanging and preserving.

Then almost as a routine, the Palmers would call a party - or perhaps rather a feast, for it was an occasion on which the pig in various guises was very much in evidence.

There was pork and ham and sausages and the delicious lard that would cover the children's bread for many a week to come. There was home-made wine and a keg of beer.

To her great satisfaction, Mrs. Palmer had somehow managed to keep the piano, now tinny-sounding and stiff, that she had played on as a young girl. It was some small piece of elegance whose memory she clutched at in the midst of the clamour of her large and chiefly male family, and the piano stood like a monument from one party to the next. Then, for one evening, it helped to transform the aspect of their labouring lives.

139

The change that such an evening brought to country neighbours and friends was astonishing. Even the least would bring some instrument that he could play, or he would memorise a monologue; more often, he would sing.

At this particular party at which George fell in love with Freda, about 20 people managed to crowd into the parlour to do justice to the meal and then to the entertainment.

To get them going, Mrs. Palmer opened the piano and played a few pieces on its dusty keys. When she got to "Love's Old Sweet Song", old Sam produced his concertina and everybody began to sing.

George's father was called on to sing "I passed by your Window" as he always did, and persuaded to add "Shipmate O' Mine" as he always was. A young lady sang delicate songs of love and death, and everybody joined in again to "Friend O' Mine".

The concertina, dulcimer and mouth organ fought on the side of the piano against the long slurred singing, but the singers won in the end with a great trailing burst that took no account of mere instruments.

There were two dramatic monologues, and George's Grandfather told the jokes that he always swore were true but had happened long ago.

But George, who was then 18, had no eyes or ears for this. His attention was engaged completely by the girl with long, golden hair that curled about her shoulders who sat demurely in a corner.

George could not take his eyes off her. When a few people stood up to try to dance a foxtrot in the small space, he went and sat beside her in the corner.

At midnight the older visitors began to search for

their walking sticks and young couples to edge out together to walk home in the moonlight. The girl shook her long curls and stood up and her mother nudged George in the back.

"Yew can walk hoom with Freda if yew like, George. Yew walk along ahid o' father an' me."

And so George did, in a dream of delight when she held out her hand for him to hold, with the golden hair touching his own shoulder and her pale face turned towards him in the moonlight.

Next day George could not rest until he had told Maudie. Maudie was the dairy-maid on the same farm. They had been to school together and he knew she was the only one who would understand how he felt. He had to tell Maudie about this wonderful girl Freda who was far too good for him.

Maudie listened and advised him in her usual commonsense way. "That on't dew to think she's tew good; yew on't git anywhere like that. Yew go along Sunday afternoon an' ask to take her out. I reckon she'll goo."

It was the first of many meetings between George and Freda. All through the spring and summer they walked out on Sunday and exchanged letters during the week. For secrecy, they did not use the post but handed their letters to Maudie who acted as go-between.

Then in the autumn, Freda's family moved away and George had further to travel and very little welcome from Freda's parents when he got there.

A farm labourer was not quite the sort of husband they envisaged for their daughter, and poor George was in despair sometimes when he went to the dairy to tell Maudie of his progress. She was indignant but said little when George told her he intended to leave the land and join the Navy in order to better himself.

As the years went by in the Navy, George kept the memory of Freda close to him and he looked forward to the day when he could claim her.

But the war intervened and he came home to a different world. His own family was scattered and the old cottage was empty in which he had once met Freda at a party. He visited the farm and the dairy, but Maudie was no longer there. In the upheaval of the war she had gone and had never returned. It was believed that she was married.

Another blow came when George discovered that Freda was married and had a baby, living not far away but now beyond reach. He rented the old cottage and set up as a market gardener and dealer, building up a prosperous business as the years passed. In his middle age he was a well-known character, considered a bit eccentric through living alone, but a man of sound judgement and responsibility.

One day, an announcement in a local paper caught his eye. For the next week he carried the cutting about with him, but refusing to accept that he could still be in love. Then at last he set pen to paper and wrote awkwardly but eloquently of his feelings.

It was to Maudie, widowed and back at the farm, that he wrote - of his sorrow, and of his desire to look after her, of his foolish blindness and of the waste of the years.

It was Maudie who rode beside him in the trap back to the cottage and who gave him in the end the solace that he sought.

Lonely Furrow

Fred was ploughing when I went along to the field with the crates of hens and a night ark on the waggon and I waited until he completed the furrow, bearing hard on the plough handles and twitching the line between his fingers as he hopped one foot in and one out of the furrow behind the horses. At the headland he pulled them to a halt and mopped his forehead, nodding towards the chicken crates.

"Are yew a-tunnin' 'em lewse, 'en?" he asked.

"They can run on the stubble for a few days, Fred. They won't be in your way".

"That they 'on't, ow partner. I'll keep an eye on 'em for yew." He came over and gave a hand to get the night ark unloaded and the hens ran squawking all over the place until they settled down to pecking at the fallen grain. Fred discovered from the huge watch in his waistcoat pocket that it was near enough time for his bait. He unhooked his bag from the collar hames and half-leaned against the tilted handles of the plough.

"The sireen ha' gone," he said, and sure enough you could hear the growing roar of the Spitfires from the aerodrome. The horses stood quietly by the hedge while Fred secured his thumb-piece and began to carve handy gobbets from it with his pocket knife. Just as the first Spitfire squadron flew over our heads barely over the tree-tops, I took my own lunch-bag from the waggon and joined Fred as he quietly spoke to the horses.

"That fare a rum 'un to me," he said, in the silence that followed, "how things fare to change for the wuss. When I was a nipper yew c'd look up there in the sky an' the wust thing that sent down 'd be a shower or a clap o' thunder. Now 'at people are more eddicated, well, there's no tellin' wha's goin' to come down."

There was the comfortable sound of anti-aircraft fire from away on the coast but no sign of the enemy. Another wave of Spitfires zoomed overhead and disappeared. "Violence," Fred commented in his gentle way, "that don't seem right, somehow, comin' from the sky. But there, 'haps tha's cos I had a dose o' that kind o' medsun long ago, I reckon."

While we sat in the mellow September sun he went on to describe how the violence of the sky came suddenly and unforgettably when he was a child.

"I warn't no more'n six or seven year old then an' I must ha' bin half asleep but I ain't ever forgot. My father, he come an' wook me up in the middle o' the night an' took me to the winder. Mother was there tew - she put suffen round me an' stood me up on the winder ledge. Tha's a sight he on't ever see agin, my father say, yew jist look out there.

Outside o' the winder there was a grut mass o' flame, a grut fire as big as a cloud an' that was a-movin' an' a-fallin'. That was one o' them German zeppelins afire an' that looked to me as if the hull sky was alight. I set up a howlin' cos I thought that was a-comin' down in the back garden. Mother say don't yew fret, she say, that on't hut yew. She oopened the

144

winder an' yew c'd hear people a-cheerin' while the zeppelin went down. When I think on't now I reckon that was the wust part o' that business - the cheerin' time the sky was full o' violence."

Fred hauled his watch out again by the chain and prepared to resume work, first of all taking the piece of bread he had saved to give to the horses. He stood by them for a minute or two in his rusty old jacket and weather-worn gaiters, smoothing the manes away from their eyes and resettling their collars to make them comfortable. Then he came back to the plough, unhurriedly lit his pipe, picked up the line and gave the word - "cubby whey, whey."

For all his love for the horses, Fred had no illusions about the dwindling value of horse ploughing. "Arter the war," he had told me more than once, "hosses 'on't be wanted any more. That'll be all tractors an' artificial manure - yew see if I ain't right."

I did not see him for the next three days, except at a distance. Then I went back to the field to move the night ark to a new site. Fred was still stumbling along behind the plough but managed to wave to indicate that he wanted to speak to me. It turned out to be he wanted to show me a brood of young pheasants he was succouring in the ditch. Then he asked if I would give him a lift as usual that evening to the village Home Guard Centre. I had almost forgotten about this and promised I would stop by his cottage at about seven o'clock. I was just turning away when old Sarah came shuffling into the field.

Fred leaned on the plough handles waiting for his wife to cross the stubble in what seemed to be old carpet slippers, her hair wispy and unkempt. I began to move away as one always did when old Sarah came by but the old man said urgently: "Don't yew go, master. Dew yew howd on a minute."

As soon as Sarah came within shouting distance she began to rail at her husband: "Where ha' yew bin? Yew ain't bin hoom. Where ha' yew bin since - since Thursday? I ain't sin yew - where ha' yew bin?"

Fred, who was known never to leave his wife's side except for the Home Guard drill, came towards her and put his hand affectionately on her arm. "Don't yew fret, ow gal," he soothed her. "I shan't leave yer. Yew goo on hoom an' make some tea - I s'all be hoom afore long."

Sarah was still peering wildly at her husband but seemed to be comforted for she said no more but turned to look at the poppies that were bright along the headland. She took a few steps towards them, then changed her mind and hurried dementedly away. I did not know what to say as we stood and watched her go.

Fred said quietly: "She ha' bin a wunnerful wife to me - an' a good mother to har children. Tha's a wicked cross to see har suffer. She git these dreadful pains in her hid, d' ye see? Haps she'll take a tarn for the better come Spring. She ain't all that bad, is she - that bad she ought to be took away?"

It was an impossible question to answer. He went on: "People say she should be put away, for har sake as well as mine. But 'course they don't know how - how good she's bin to me. She was a lovely gal long ago - I felt like a king a-walkin' out with her in our courtin' days. I cou'n't stand by now an' see har put away. Arter all, I can still manage to comfort her a bit

146

when we're togither."

Before I could think of something to reply he shook the plough line and was off again, bearing on the handles to keep the furrow straight - afraid, it seemed to me, to hear what I would answer.

That evening I got out the car for what was considered an 'essential journey' and went into the village by the back lane in order to pick Fred up. Usually he waited for me at the gate of the cottage looking awkward but still retaining an air of simple dignity in the Home Guard uniform, as honestly loyal to the idea of protecting the village as he was to his horses and to his wife.

Tonight he was not to be seen. When I sounded the horn there was a long pause and then at last he came slowly round from the back of the cottage. He was not in his uniform but was wearing his Sunday best suit and hat. He came along the garden path so slowly I thought he must be ill and I got out of the car to meet him as he reached the gate. He put his hands on the gate and looked past me as if he were dreaming.

"Tell the sergeant - tell him I shan't be a-comin'. Tha's Sarah," He faltered as his head dropped on his hands. "I ha' put Sarah to sleep, she had sech a lot o' pain I cou'n't see har suffer no more."

I saw then other figures coming from the back of the cottage, gawping, awestruck neighbours and behind, the village constable, still holding a handkerchief to his face. He came up to the gate, coughing.

"I shall have to take yew away, Fred," he said mildly. "Yew know that, don't yew?" Fred nodded.

"I made har right comfortable afore I tunned the

147

gas on. That din't hut har a mite. I jest put har to sleep. She 'on't suffer no more."

He pulled on the coat that someone had brought from the house. "There's jest the animals -" he turned to me apologetically - my rabbits an' my chickens. Don't let them poor things go hungry."